G000252271

CONTENTS

LIST OF ILLUSTRATIONS

(between pp. 14 and 15)

The author wishes to acknowledge Robert Chapman of Plymouth for Plates I, IV, VI, VII, VIII a), X, XI, XII, XIII a) and b); Nicholas Toyne of Newton Abbot for Plates III, V, IX; and Waverley Photographics of Barnstaple for Plate II. The map and pedigree have been drawn by Mr. Rodney Fry.

FOREWORD

When one considers the eminence of the Acland family and their long history in Devon it is amazing that only Lady Acland, the author of this book, has tackled the subject. They are probably, if not certainly, the oldest surviving landed family in the county. Their name first occurs in a deed dated 1155, when they were holding land—not a large area—in North Devon in the vicinity of Barnstaple. Since then they have had a continuous existence without a change of name. Lady Acland has written this book with charm and as a result of prolonged labours among records of all kinds.

A subject which interests me particularly is where did these feudal families below the rank of the aristocracy come from? The answer, to my mind, is that the Aclands, under another name which we do not know, came over from Flanders at or soon after the so-called Norman Conquest. We tend to forget that although the Normans played by far the largest part in the Conquest they were aided to a considerable degree by Flemings and Picards whose motives probably were mainly the plunder of England. The Normans obtained, as we know, by far the largest share, but the Flemings also received their reward for being on the successful side. The evidence for this statement, so far as the Aclands are concerned, is that they first appear in a corner of North Devon close to the village of Bratton Fleming. The other clue is a tenuous one, but in this early period of feudal history we have to seize upon every clue. In this case it is the marked tendency for the Aclands of the twelfth and thirteenth centuries to adopt the Christian name of Baldwin. Now the powerful counts of Flanders also favoured this Christian name and it occurs over and over again in their early pedigree. So it does also in the early generations of the Acland pedigree, and this can be no accident. I think the relationship was probably that those Flemings who crossed over to England retained the Christian name of Baldwin and that the Aclands also kept the name for several generations. Probably they were military followers of the counts of Flanders on the other side of the Channel and kept the name Baldwin when they reached England.

There are traces of Flemish influence in the place-names of this part of Devon. Technically the Aclands ranked as sokemen, which is below the level of knight, but well up the social scale. They were endowed by their lords with a modest estate of land as their primary function was to aid their lord in warlike enterprise. So I suggest that the Aclands, before they came to Devon, were one of the numerous families who either fought at Hastings on the Norman side or followed along soon afterwards.

At any rate, they settled on a small estate which had belonged at some date to one Acca, and as a result of this their surname became Acland and never changed again. On this land they flourished quietly, rarely engaged in warfare. Their own good fortune was what we might call genetic in that they never failed in the male line and always produced a son or two to carry on. Those families who were unfortunate enough to produce only daughters saw their lands disappear into other hands in the form of dowries at marriage and so their names perished. The Aclands never suffered this misfortune and they look like continuing their good fortune into the indefinite future.

At one time in the nineteenth century they had accumulated an enormous estate of practically 40,000 acres, and exerted great influence in Devon both in the north and the east of the county. In this period they produced some giants among landowners, whose career Lady Acland sketches in a fascinating way. Their name lives on, but their huge estates have passed mainly to the National Trust.

W. G. HOSKINS

Exeter, 1981

INTRODUCTION AND ACKNOWLEDGEMENTS

I have written this book because I have been a member of the Acland family for 45 years, and during that time I have accumulated so much information about its history that it seemed a pity not to use it. I should never have begun the task if it had not been suggested by Professor Hoskins, at a chance meeting about twenty years ago, and later urged upon me by my family as a gentle occupation for my retirement. In fact, it has proved to be quite as hard as anything which I attempted during my professional life, and my lack of progress has been the despair of everybody concerned, including my patient publishers.

There are two omissions which I much regret. I wish that I had been able to write more fully about the branches which came from the parent tree in the nineteenth century, and in particular those which began with Henry Wentworth and John Barton; they have flourished so vigorously that they need separate histories of their own. In addition to this, the flat, factual postscript may disappoint readers who would have liked to see the story of the Aclands brought up to date. To carry the narrative into the present—and perhaps later—would certainly involve a change in the approach and the objective attitude which I have tried to adopt in the present volume. There is plenty of material for future family historians who want to make good these shortcomings.

Apart from Professor Hoskins, who has been my mainstay throughout, I am grateful to everybody who has encouraged me to persevere with my writing, and especially to Mollie Dexter, who has not only edited this book, but has much improved it.

I could have done very little without the Devon Record Office, which holds most of the Acland papers on permanent loan. I offer my best thanks to all the archivists, both past and present, belonging to this splendid Office; not only have they expertly sorted and listed a muddled mass of documents, but they have also given me unfailing help in extracting the information which I needed. Exeter is rich in good libraries, and I have made use of them all. From a list of invariably kind librarians I must single out Mr. Geoffrey Paley, to whom all awkward queries about the West Country can safely be referred. On particular aspects of my subject I have been much helped by Bishop Wilfrid Westall, Mr. J. K. Ridler, Dr. Harold Harley, and the officials of the Saratoga National Park in New York State. The Earl of Harrowby, Mr. Napier Collyns, and Mr. Tony Scotland have allowed me to quote from their papers. I am grateful to them all.

Lastly, I thank my own family for their patient encouragement, even when my progress was slow. To them and all the Acland cousins this book properly belongs.

ANNE ACLAND

Sprydon, 1981

Chapter One

ACLAND BARTON (1155–1553)

The Tudor Portrait (Plate I)

THE TUDOR PORTRAIT of John Acland of Acland is the oldest, and for that reason one of the most cherished, in the family collection. Painted in the middle of the sixteenth century, it shows a man in early middle age standing slightly sideways against a dark background, his hands firmly grasping a pair of gloves, and his brown eyes turned to face the spectator with an air of quiet confidence, as if he were well aware of the trouble and expense involved in sitting for his portrait and quite satisfied that it was worth it. He wears a black velvet cap, a black doublet with narrow white lace at the collar and cuffs, and a black gown with a fur-lined cape, while on his capable hands are two plain gold rings. With his prosperous, yet somehow provincial appearance he might be a minor Tudor official or simply a country gentleman who wanted his portrait painted for posterity. If so, his trouble has been recompensed, for his portrait has looked down on 16 generations of his direct descendants already, and there is every indication that it will do so for a long time yet.

Because he is the first of the family to emerge from the shadows of history as a visible human being, it comes almost as a shock to realise that far from being one of the earliest ancestors, he appears almost exactly midway in the family pedigree. Aclands had been living at Acland for at least four hundred years before the Tudor portrait was painted.

The Beginning

The story begins in the North Devon parish of Landkey, near Barnstaple, where the western edge of Exmoor slopes

1

steeply down to the basin of the Taw and its tributaries. Here, in 1155, Hugh de Accalen is recorded as owning land. 'Acland', no matter how it is spelt, means 'Acca's lane'[1] and refers to a Saxon, Acca, who—judging from other place-names—once owned a sizeable estate in this district. Acland stands well up out of the Landkey valley, at a height of 400ft. above sea level, looking out across the Taw estuary and, as Risdon remarked in 1600, 'pleasantly situated against the south in the side of a hill which hath given name to its ancient dwellers'. Shelter is still one of the best assets of Acland, and with modern implements and fertilisers farming thrives there today, but it must have been a hard job to cultivate the soil with medieval tools when the Aclands settled at the end of Acca's long lane and made Acland Barton their home.

Where they came from in the beginning is a mystery. There are pointers towards a Flemish origin, which Professor Hoskins has touched on in his foreword. It must have been for some good reason that the family chose the favourite Flemish name of Baldwin at least five times out of the first eight generations which followed Hugh: certainly, the fact was unusual enough to rate a mention by Sir William Pole, Devon's first historian, in the seventeenth century. By the end of the twelfth century the Aclands were holding an estate of about 400 acres from the Bishop of Exeter by a form of tenure called 'socage', which, as Professor Hoskins explains, put them on a social level just below that of a knight. Thus they were virtually freeholders from the time they settled in north Devon.

Natural Increase

We know little about the medieval Aclands except the bare facts of marriage, death, and the transfer of property which are contained in attested pedigrees and the scanty legal documents which survive. For a couple of hundred years they seem to have been simply the trusted, well-respected men of their neighbourhood, likely to be called upon as witnesses or jurymen, and ready to pay their taxes or take arms for the king when required. There are no heroic deeds to record: when Sir William Pole made out his list of 'Persons of Most Note in War and Peace' in 1600, the only Acland whom he found worthy

of being included in it was John, who went to France in 1386
to fight for Richard II in the Hundred Years' War, as a mere
man-at-arms. The Aclands' real talent was for survival in the
male line, and in this they were unsurpassed. The remarkable
ability to produce sons, which Professor Hoskins has mentioned,
enabled them to marry heiresses of neighbouring estates who
brought their land as dowry into the Acland patrimony and
lifted the family up the social ladder. Younger brothers—of
whom there was usually a plentiful supply—became lesser landowners, merchants and clergy, and from these are descended
the many Aclands in Devon and elsewhere, who spell their
name with 'k'. The main line dropped it altogether in the
eighteenth century. However the name is spelt, there is no
branch of the enormous family which does not stem from the
tree which first took root at Acland Barton.

The original house was completely rebuilt in the fifteenth
century, with its own domestic chapel, licensed by the bishop
to save the family a muddy walk to Landkey in the winter
(Plate II). This in itself was a sign that the Aclands had entered
the class of the gentry; their wives, by now, were beginning to
bring heraldic arms with them as well as property, and the new
estates came from further afield. Though Acland Barton has been
a farmhouse now for many generations, the solidity of that late
medieval prosperity still makes itself felt in the impressive
screened entrance passage and the dusty carvings of the chapel
roof. The date 1591 carved on the porch marks a later alteration.

With the Tudors the Aclands' steady progress up the social
scale continued. They never benefited directly from the Dissolution of the Monasteries—even though some of the new wealth
came to them later through marriage—but, as landowners, they
shared in the general prosperity which was making Devon into
one of the most valuable counties in the English economy
through its cloth and fishing industries. The population rose,
farming flourished, and much marginal land came into cultivation. By the 1550s when John Acland of Acland sat for his
portrait, he owned land in the parishes of Loxbeare, Chittlehampton, Tedburn St. Mary, High Bray, and Swimbridge, and
bore heraldic arms of his own. So far had four hundred years of
natural increase brought the family from its modest beginnings.

Chapter Two

COLUMB JOHN AND KILLERTON (1553-1728)

The Move to the South

JOHN, WHO HAD made a good marriage to the daughter of
Hugh Radcliff of Stepney and the Middle Temple, died in
1553[1] leaving two sons, Hugh and John, whose lives ran in
parallel throughout the reigns of Mary and Elizabeth and well
into the time of James I. Hugh remained all his life at Acland
Barton and, in due course, married Margaret Monk from the
Devon family who was one day to produce the great general.
John, the younger brother, moved south and bought the manor
of Columb John in the parish of Broadclyst, once the property
of the Earls of Devon. Here he rebuilt the old house and its
domestic chapel in a manner which, according to Westcote,
the contemporary topographer, gave it 'a fairer lustre than
before'. It was probably his marriage to a member of the Rolle
family—all of them great beneficiaries from the Dissolution of
the Monasteries—which made the purchase possible in the first
place, but, once at Columb John, he took root and flourished
more vigorously than his elder brother ever did in north Devon.
The richer soil and milder climate may have accounted for this,
as well as a second prosperous marriage to a widowed daughter
of the Portman family. At all events, he was an established
figure by the end of Elizabeth's reign: a justice of the peace
for Devon, twice in parliament, sheriff when his turn came
round, and rich enough to acquire a knighthood when needy
James I came to the throne. Having no children from either of
his marriages he was able to give largely to charity: £800 for
a fine new dining-hall at Exeter College, Oxford, with two
scholarships for poor students—the first of their kind at that
college—as well as money to give bread to the poor in every one

4

of the 27 parishes in which he possessed land. Well before he died in 1620, John Acland commissioned a handsome monument of himself for Broadclyst church, in the fashionable Renaissance style and there he lies in his knightly armour with a widow kneeling at his head and feet, his passage to Heaven assured, maybe, as much by his proximity to the altar as by his numerous benefactions to the needy (Plate III). As an inscription in another Devon church puts it:[2]

> Here Sr John Acland to the poor's a friend,
> In giving bread, noe times to have an end.
> Sixpence a week by him to us is measured.
> A crown for him in Heaven's laid up and treasured.

Hugh Acland was over seventy when his brother died, and he only survived him by two years. He lived the life of a country gentleman and a justice of the peace, making no particular mark in North Devon, but prospering well enough to modernise Acland Barton in 1591, and to put up an impressive monument in Landkey church to his only son, Arthur, who died as a young man. The inscription describes, in 'impolisht verse', Arthur's knighthood and his marriage to Eleanor Malet, who bore him a son. It was this boy—another John—who inherited doubly from his grandfather and great-uncle, and who in 1622 decided to move south and make Columb John the main family seat, leaving Acland Barton as a house for younger branches.

The Troubles

By this time England had been ruled for nearly twenty years by James I, and was fast losing the spirit of national unity which had been so carefully fostered by Elizabeth. With her unique gift for compromise she had managed to contain widely different religious opinions within a single English Church, while at the same time holding crown and parliament together in a working partnership. James had nothing of this quality. His passionate conviction that the divine right of kings gave him leave to ride roughshod over the opinions of his subjects was made even less attractive by his singular lack of tact and personal charm. He had recently been at loggerheads with parliament over the question of his authority—tearing a page out of the Commons journal with his own hand because it contained a formal protest—and he refused to hear of any religion which did not conform to Bishop Laud's rigid churchmanship: it was at this very time that the Pilgrim Fathers set sail from Plymouth in the *Mayflower* to escape from persecution. Prince Charles, the heir to the throne, seemed likely to be even less tolerant when his turn came. Thus, even before John Acland was well established at Columb John, the scene was set for the struggle which, 20 years later, divided Devon into royalists and parliamentarians.

There were now two Acland properties in Broadclyst parish. The manor of Killerton, which adjoined Columb John, had been bought as a jointure for John's widowed mother, and she continued to live there after her second marriage to Sir Francis Vincent, who had a daughter of his own, named Elizabeth. The two houses were only a mile apart and visits between them must have been frequent: certainly on wet Sundays in winter the Killerton party went over to Columb John chapel to hear divine service read by the family chaplain, just as Bishop Cotton of Exeter had intended when he allowed the consecration of the building on account of 'the distance from the Parish Church, the occasional overflowing of the waters and the bad state of the roads'. In due course John Acland married his step-sister, Elizabeth Vincent, and by the time the Civil War broke out they had six children under 10 years old, five of them boys. Elizabeth's portrait (Plate IV) shows her as a charming but determined young woman with her hair dressed in the becoming style of Charles I's queen, Henrietta Maria, as if to make it quite clear that the family was royalist. Why, it is impossible to say. The squires of Devon were pretty evenly split—Acland's nearest neighbour, Sir John Bampfylde, was a leading parliamentarian—and some families, like the Fortescues, were divided even among themselves. Personal loyalty to the king came into it, no doubt, but so did firm church principles: Bishop Cotton, who had been a family friend until he died at Silverton, was a strongly anti-Puritan follower of Laud, and there is evidence that the vicar of Broadclyst shared his views. For whatever reason, John Acland was a very active Cavalier when the country was called to arms in the summer of 1642.

At the start of the war, parliament was firmly in control of Devon through the existing local militia, efficiently organised by the Lord Lieutenant. The king tried to raise his own local armies by issuing sympathisers like Acland with 'Commissions of Array', giving them authority to enlist troops, but the attempt was a failure. Even Acland—himself a colonel of militia in north Devon, who could call upon tenants for help all over the county—found it hopeless to recruit these 'array men', and, like many other royalists in Devon, he submitted for the time being to parliamentary rule, probably praying for some peaceful compromise. The Cornish were much keener for the king. Under Sir Ralph Hopton, they formed an army which was bold enough to venture into Devon in the autumn of 1642, with the intention of besieging Exeter. They found a brave and useful ally in John Acland, who was glad to garrison his house for the king and to gallop up to North Devon at the head of 500 soldiers in order to get hold of his old militia men and threaten Barnstaple; he got no further than Torrington, however, before he was forced back home, to find that the siege of Exeter had failed and that Hopton was on his way back to Cornwall for the winter. When the Cornish army returned in the spring, after a famous victory at Stratton, near the border, it passed quickly eastwards on its way to get help from the main royalist forces in Dorset and Somerset. As Clarendon, the royalist historian, wrote, Devon was left 'in a very unsafe posture; there being only a small party at Columb John, a house of Sir John Acland's, three miles off Exeter, to control the power of that city . . . and to dispute not only with any commotion that might happen in the country, but with any power that might arrive by sea'.

During 1643, the royalist position improved, and by the late summer, when help came in the person of the king's nephew, Prince Maurice, at the head of half the king's army, Columb John was no longer an isolated outpost. Many more royalists had declared themselves openly, and some notable parliamentarians had changed sides, including the Earl of Bedford, the Lord Lieutenant of Exeter and Devon. Exeter's corporation had been put to great expense in order to repair the city's fortifications against continual royalist skirmishes,

and were probably only too glad to call off the siege. At all
events, when the prince arrived he had no trouble in taking,
without bloodshed, 'that rich and pleasant city' as Clarendon
called it 'which had suffered no other distress or impression
from the besiegers than the being kept from taking the air
without their own walls, and from being supplied from the
country markets'. With the exception of valiant Plymouth—
the only town in Devon never to change hands in the course
of the war—the whole of the county was in royalist control
by the end of the year.

Everywhere, except in the West Country, things were going
badly for the king. In May 1644 he sent the queen down to
Exeter for the birth of her fifth child, in order to be, as Clarendon said, 'in a place out of the reach of any alarm', but by the
middle of the summer, when Princess Henrietta was barely a
fortnight old, news came of an impending parliamentarian
invasion of the West and the mother was so distressed that she
travelled down to Falmouth to embark for her native France.
When the king arrived in Exeter in July he found his new
daughter in charge of a lady-in-waiting at the Earl of Bedford's
great town house. With the 15-year-old Prince of Wales lodged
at the Deanery, Exeter was dominated by the Court circle that
summer. Loyal subjects had every opportunity to show their
appreciation in the way that Charles expected, and the goldsmiths of the city were kept busy melting down plate at a
mint set up in the castle.[3] The Acland family silver probably
went this way, for there was none of it left when the war
was over.

The king's object in coming to the West was to pursue the
Earl of Essex, who was leading a parliamentarian expedition
down the length of the peninsula—apparently convinced that
it would be welcomed as an army of liberation. In this he was
much mistaken. Response in Devon was very mixed, and, as
for the Cornish, the further he went into their narrow county
the more fiercely royalist he found them. When the king and
Prince Maurice finally caught up with him at Lostwithiel he
realised that there was no way out except by sea, and he took
a boat from Fowey rather than surrender, leaving his troops
to get away as best they could. King Charles rode back

victorious and reached Exeter on 13 September. It must have been one of his last cheerful moments. During the four days which he spent in the city before returning towards his Oxford headquarters he conferred several knighthoods on those who had helped him. There was, too, a single baronetcy for John Acland, whom he also appointed as sheriff of the county. Perhaps the honour was a just reward for generosity, but it is pleasant to think that King Charles remembered the solitary Columb John garrison of the year before.

When the king rode away from the West most of the glamour of the war went with him. His supporters were left to face their third dark, wet Devon war-time winter, with stocks of money and food running very short, and morale at a low ebb. Army commanders quarrelled among themselves, unpaid soldiers stole without compunction, and many sane people must have longed only for the war to be over. Sir John Acland, whose presence as sheriff was often needed in Exeter, had a house in the city—commandeered from a parliamentarian merchant named Richard Evans—where he kept a good deal of his military equipment, including a field bedstead, 14 leather trunks, and a 'Great Mappe of England' which must have been indispensable for interpreting the news of the war. News was not good that winter. While the king kept to his Oxford headquarters, the parliamentary cause was taking on an entirely new moral and physical strength through the formation of the New Model Army under Fairfax and Cromwell. When it emerged, fully fledged, in the spring of 1645—a disciplined force of picked professional soldiers, properly paid out of the taxes and led by officers of strong Puritan principles—it was clear that the divided and penniless royalist troops could never stand against it, and when the fatal news from Naseby made that hitherto unknown spot the chief centre of attention on Sir John's great map of England, everybody knew that the war was as good as over.

Exeter prepared itself for a siege, waiting for the New Model Army to come to the West. Fairfax, followed by Cromwell, appeared in Devon in October, and with surprise and relief most people found that the new soldiers were a civilised lot, who paid for what they took, and that the new officers knew how to behave like gentlemen even to their enemies. So at least thought Lady Acland after Fairfax and Cromwell had made Columb John their headquarters: 'I received such ample testimony of your love when you were pleased to quarter at my house as that I cannot sufficiently express my thankfulness for the same', she wrote to Cromwell. Perhaps Sir John, who was part of the Exeter garrison, thought the same after a winter of siege. Then the two generals came back to Columb John from a victorious campaign in Devon and Cornwall and offered such reasonable terms to the city that on 13 April 1646 all soldiers and civilians who so wished were able to march out with colours flying and go free, provided that they laid down their arms and took the national covenant of loyalty. Prominent 'delinquents' were to be fined, but on a lesser scale than ordinary if they paid up quickly. In Sir John Acland's case the fine was fixed at 10 per cent. of the rental value of his property, and came to £1,727—the fourth largest in Devon. He was prompt in submitting a detailed valuation to the Committee for Compounding, which sat at Goldsmiths' Hall in London, and by 4 August half the fine was paid and the remainder secured to the Committee's satisfaction. However, that was not the end of it: it was a great time for settling old scores, and, once Fairfax and Cromwell had marched away, the Parliamentary Commissioners who were left in charge were much less merciful. Richard Evans in particular was determined to get his revenge. He bombarded Goldsmiths' Hall with complaints of Acland's 'inveterate malice and cruel commands' in taking over the Exeter house, insisted that the valuation of his estate was false, and claimed that as a particularly malignant royalist he deserved to be fined at a higher rate. Accordingly a new valuation was made (admittedly there were some remarkable discrepancies), and a new fine was fixed at nearly three times the original amount. This would certainly have meant the sale of a substantial portion of the Acland estates, but before the matter could be settled circumstances had changed in a way which resulted in a more generous decision.

By April 1648 there was a new Sir John Acland to make out his case. He was 13 years old, and amazingly enough, the third baronet, for in less than two years both his parents as well as his elder brother had died, leaving this young boy as the head of the family. He by-passed Goldsmiths' Hall and wrote straight to the House of Commons describing his situation: the pathetic letter begs for clemency and time to pay off the rest of his debt 'whereby himself and three younger brothers and sister, being all very young, may be preserved from ruin'.[4] Luckily parliament was less vengeful than Richard Evans, and the fine was settled in the lesser sum. The chapter was closed, but a generation later there was a pleasant family postscript to the Civil War when the 1st baronet's grand-daughter, Margaret, married the Earl of Arundell, of Trerice in Cornwall. He was a grandson of the magnificent Sir John Arundell ('Jack for the King') who, as the octogenarian governor of Pendennis Castle, had been the last man in the West of England to hold out for Charles I. The union between these two old royalist families was one day to bring the beautiful Cornish property of Trerice into the Acland empire.

After King Charles I had been executed in January 1649, 12 years of experimental government ensued, first with a monarchy under the Commonwealth, and then without a parliament under the Protectorate—neither one of them suiting the English temperament any better than the Puritan suppression of pleasure which went with it. At last in 1660 parliament and the monarchy were both restored by popular demand and, for the time at least, some sort of partnership was restored between the two. All through these distracting years the Aclands were chiefly concerned with the business of survival, and, if they privately thought that God and the Commonwealth were on opposite sides, they were probably too occupied with their own troubles to care. Burial registers all over Devon point to the epidemics which broke out during this period. Five members of the Acland family died in 1655, including young Sir John himself, one of his brothers, and both his small sons, one of whom survived him for a few weeks as the infant 4th Baronet. So it came about that Hugh Acland, the fourth son of the 1st Baronet of Columb John, became the fifth holder of the family title only eight years after his father's death. Once more an ample provision of males had enabled the family to survive.

The Two Hughs

'Hugh the Fifth' as he is called by his descendants—18 when he inherited—lived to be 76 and saw the family fortunes rise from their lowest ebb to something approaching full flood in the first decade of the eighteenth century. Even after the whole of the Commissioners' fine had been paid, all the land was still intact, though some of it was no doubt mortgaged. Hugh's financial position was eased when he married Ann Daniel, the daughter of a prosperous Yorkshire knight, who brought him a dowry as well as bearing him four sons and two daughters. By 1677 he was rich enough to pay Charles II a fee of £1,095 for new letters patent to confirm the baronetcy—the originals having been destroyed in 'the distractions of the late times'— and to celebrate the event by sitting for his portrait to the fashionable Court painter, Sir Peter Lely.

At a by-election in the following year he became one of the two members of parliament for Tiverton Borough and sat in the House of Commons through the crowded 10-year period which saw the end of Charles II's reign, the brief and disastrous appearance on the throne of his Catholic brother, James II, and finally the direct appeal from a group of influential Englishmen, which brought the Protestant Prince William of Orange across the Channel from Holland to rule the country with his Stuart bride, Mary—herself firmly Protestant. A two-party system had begun to emerge in the House, and men who had once called themselves parliamentarians and royalists now used the new slang terms of 'Whig' and 'Tory'.[5] Hugh was naturally a Tory, but at this particular time both the parties were united in a determination to keep England Protestant and to free themselves from monarchs who believed in their divine right to rule, regardless of the people's will. Indeed, for seven out of these 10 years parliament was prorogued or dissolved altogether, by Charles and James successively, in an effort to get their own way. Once the Act of Settlement in 1689 had put William and Mary firmly on the throne and brought about political and religious stability such as had not been seen since the days of Elizabeth, the Whig party predominated in parliament, and Hugh the Fifth was not returned again for Tiverton.

His life now centred on Killerton, which in 1680 he had altered and enlarged to make it the principal family mansion, in preference to Columb John. He may well have used some of the stonework from that house, for it was taken down at about this date. The chapel was left and furnished with a new silver chalice[6] to replace one which had disappeared during the Troubles, but only an archway remained to mark, as it still does, the place where Fairfax and Cromwell had once ridden to quarter at Columb John (Plate V).

Hugh the Fifth died in 1713 and was succeeded by his grandson who, confusingly enough, bore the same Christian name. Hugh the Sixth is chiefly remembered for his splendid marriage. He was no public figure, and though he was briefly in parliament as Tory member for Barnstaple during Queen Anne's reign—the year of the South Sea Bubble—there is no indication that he spoke on that or any other subject.

His marriage in 1721 to Cecily Wroth, elder daughter and co-heiress of Sir Thomas Wroth of Petherton Park in Somerset, brought into Acland possession the 2,300 acres near Bridgwater together with a cash endowment of £12,000, and a handsome set of portraits of the Wroth, Palmer and Vernai families, all of whose fortunes had flowed into Cecily's dowry. It was a magnificent match which much hastened the Aclands' return to prosperity.

A curious anecdote about Hugh appeared in *The Gentleman's Magazine,* and although many times reproduced in other journals, it has never been contradicted:

A remarkable Fact to prevent sudden Interments

The late Sir Hugh Ackland of Devonshire, apparently died of a fever, and was laid out as dead: the nurse, with two of the footmen, sat up with the corpse. Lady Ackland sent them a bottle of brandy to drink in the night: one of the servants, being an arch rogue, told the other, that his master dearly loved brandy when he was alive, and, says he, I am resolved he shall drink one glass with us now he is dead; the fellow accordingly poured out a bumper of brandy, and forced it down his throat: a guggling immediately ensued, and a violent motion of the neck and upper part of the breast. The other footman and the nurse were so terrified, that they ran down stairs; and the brandy genius, hastening away with rather too much speed, tumbled down stairs head foremost. The noise of the fall, and his cries, alarmed a young gentleman who slept in the house that night; who got up, and went to the room where the corpse lay, and, to his great surprise, saw Sir Hugh sitting upright. He called the servants; Sir Hugh was put into a warm bed, and the physician and apothecary sent for. These gentlemen, in a few weeks, perfectly restored their patient to health, and he lived several years afterwards.

The above story is well known to the Devonshire people; as in most companies Sir Hugh used to tell this strange circumstance, and to talk of his resurrection by his brandy footman, to whom (when he really died) he left a handsome annuity.

Sir Hugh's will contains no mention of the brandy footman to confirm the veracity of the anecdote, but it is so evocative of its robust period that it must be allowed to stand, although Hugh the Sixth really died in 1728.

I. John Acland of Acland (artist unknown).

III.   The tomb of Sir John Acland, Knight, in Broadclyst church.

IV. Lady Acland, wife of Sir John Acland, 1st Baronet of Columb John (artist unknow

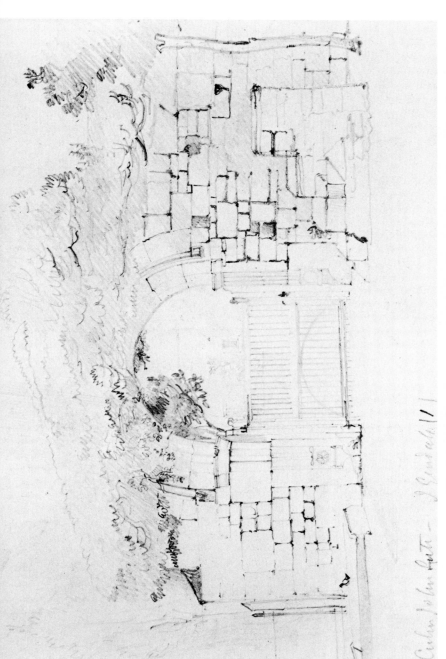

V.   The gate at Columb John; a pencil sketch by John Gendall, c. 1840.

VI. Sir Thomas Dyke Acland, 7th Baronet (1723-1785); a portrait by Sir Joshua Reyno

II. Elizabeth Dyke, who married Sir Thomas Acland, 7th Baronet, in 1745, and added
er name to that of his family (artist unknown).

VIII.   a) Holnicote House before the fire of 1779; the new house was built in another position. North Hill is behind the house, and the Bristol Channel is in the distance. Allerford can be seen on the left, and Selworthy on the right (artist unknown).

VIII.   b) Killerton House and Park: an aquatint from a drawing by L. E. Reed, 1819.

IX. Lady Harriet Acland's journey down the Hudson River; an engraving published in 1784, taken from an oil painting exhibited at the Royal Academy in 1778. A good deal of licence has been taken by the artist.

X. 'The Great Sir Thomas' Acland, 10th Baronet (1787-1871). The portrait was paint
by William Owen in 1818, and was presented to Lady Acland in 1818 by Acland's Tor
Committee as a consolation for his defeat in the election of that year. The Exe estuary
be seen behind the walls of Exeter Castle, the place of voting. Acland holds the notes
a speech in his hand.

Lydia, wife of 'The Great Sir Thomas', with her sons Tom, aged five, and Arthur,
d three. The portrait was painted in 1814 by Sir Thomas Lawrence to celebrate Lydia's
overy from an illness. The background shows the Exe valley beyond Killerton Clump.

XII.   'The Great Sir Thomas' as an old man, photographed in 1867 by Harry Thorn at Bu
The seal on his key-ring is still in use by his great-great grandson, Richard.

XIII.   a) (*left*) Thomas Dyke Acland (1809-1898), later 11th Baronet, by George Richmond, 1856.

XIII.   b) (*below*) Mary Erskine, drawn in 1856 by George Richmond on her marriage to Thomas Dyke Acland as his second wife.

XIV. Sir Thomas Dyke Acland, 11th Baronet, photographed *c.* 1890 as an old man.

XV. The two brothers, drawn by F. C. Gould, the sub-editor and caricaturist of *The Westminster Gazette*.

a) (*left*) Sir Charles Thomas Dyke Acland, 12th Baronet (1842-1919). This drawing was presented to him by the artist on the occasion of his silver wedding anniversary in 1905.

b) (*below*) Arthur Herbert Dyke Acland, later 13th Baronet (1847-1926). A political cartoon drawn in 1893, when Arthur was in the Cabinet and was struggling to raise the standard of Church School buildings. The Bishop of Salisbury, who sponsored an Elementary Education (Religious Instruction) Bill in that year, is shown holding Arthur back with 'manacles'.

XVI. Lloyd George at Killerton in 1926. Here he launched his Land Policy at a rally of 19,000 people in the Park. From left

Chapter Three

THE PEAK OF PROSPERITY AND THE SPORTING
SQUIRES (1728–1794)

SIR HUGH ACLAND died as a young man in 1728, and his
five-year-old son, Thomas, inherited the property and title as
7th Baronet (Plate VI). He had two younger brothers and a
sister to keep him company, and within a short time his mother,
Cecily, made a second marriage to Thomas Troyte, the family
chaplain, and produced two step-brothers. The Troytes lived at
Killerton, and the children grew up there together. Thomas,
however, moved to the Somerset property when he came of
age in 1744, and made his home at Petherton Park. He was
already a rich man, with two estates to choose from, and he
followed the example of his father by marrying, in 1745, a
wife who was richer still. Elizabeth Dyke of Tetton, near
Taunton, was sole heiress to her father and uncle, both of
whom had accumulated large estates from the Blackford and
Dyke families. The marriage heralded an era when the prosperity of the Acland family rose to its highest peak. 'Fine
woman, Miss Dyke!' the estate bailiff is supposed to have
exclaimed, and, indeed, she does look a fine woman in her
portrait, with her head held high and her face glowing with
health and vigour (Plate VII). The compliment, however, was
intended in a different sense. Even a glance at the Acland-Dyke
marriage settlement is enough to show that Elizabeth was also
a very fine woman in terms of worldly goods—though much
more than a glance is needed to disentangle the details of her
possessions from the bundle of huge, closely-written documents
which record the transaction. Sir Thomas found himself master
of three separate new estates in Somerset, based on three family
houses at Holnicote, near Porlock (Plate VIII a), Pixton, near

15

Dulverton, and Tetton, near Taunton. The land extended
into 24 parishes, and there was also a substantial sum of money
in securities. The lawyers considered the settlement 'to amount
to thirty thousand pounds or thereabouts', and all this now
came into Acland ownership as an addition to the existing
family estates at Killerton, near Exeter, and Petherton Park,
near Bridgwater. It was a condition of inheritance that Elizabeth Dyke should add her surname to that of her husband, and
there was a legal discussion as to whether 'Acland-Dyke' or
'Dyke-Acland' was the proper form. The advice of Richard
Cridland, the family man of business, was not enough. An
Exeter lawyer, Mr. Cholwich (later Recorder of the city) 'was
called on for an opinion': on the whole, he rather preferred the
first version. Sir Thomas, however, thought differently and
got his way. He stuck to his own surname, inserting 'Dyke'
in front of it with no hyphen, and this has remained the family
usage in the main line ever since.

Apart from the splendid dowry and the added name, the
marriage had a further important effect on the family. Holnicote and Pixton estates, both on the verge of Exmoor, included
great stretches of the finest stag-hunting country in England,
and—uniquely in the Acland story—hunting now became an
absorbing passion. In no period does sport of any kind merit
more than a passing mention except in this one half century
when it coloured the lives of the 7th Baronet and his son
(another Thomas) so intensely as to earn them the description
of 'sporting squires'. The elder Thomas typified, in many ways,
that class of West-Country landowner which was substantial and
influential without being among the very wealthiest. The middle
of the eighteenth century was a period when news of battles
abroad or corruption at Westminster troubled Devon and
Somerset very little. To serve as a member of parliament was a
duty to be undertaken and not a privilege to be sought, even
though the invitation might be welcomed as a mark of honour.
Many squires could remember, as Sir Thomas could, that their
grandfathers or great-grandfathers had fought in the Civil War,
and feel thankful that peaceful times now made it possible for
them to husband their estates, rebuild and re-furnish their
houses when they wished to, and, above all, to enjoy their

possessions to the fullest possible extent. It was no shame to drink, gamble, cockfight, or beget children out of wedlock. The 7th Baronet did all these things, and yet died as well respected as any man in the West of England.

He was invited to stand for parliament very soon after his marriage. Devon was a single constituency, returning two members who, at that time, were Sir William Courtenay and Theophilus Fortescue, representatives of the two greatest families in the county. Fortescue died early in 1746, and Acland was asked to take his place. There was no opposition, but he wrote to friends and relations asking for support. Lord Clinton politely declined. John Parker of Saltram had been intending to stand himself, but withdrew in a friendly spirit; warm replies came from Sir John Trevelyn of Nettlecombe, J. F. Buller of Morval, Sir John Pole of Shute, A. Champerowne of Dartington, John Yonge of Puslynch and a number of others. Mr. Wyndham of Newhouse was a 'kinsman', John Acland a cousin from the North Devon branch. W. Stevens of Winscott would 'readily have waited on' Sir Thomas on polling day in Exeter, 'but as the smallpox are said to be much there and neither myself wife or children past ye disorder, hope you'll excuse me'. Acland was duly elected to represent Devon, but there is no indication that he ever had any taste for London or politics, and when a general election came in 1747 he did not stand again.

Lady Acland did not live long to enjoy her married life. She died in May 1753, having borne two sons, John in January 1747, and Thomas in April 1752. The dates hint at a death in child-birth, and possible previous miscarriages: perhaps she was less robust than her portrait suggests. At all events, at the age of 29, Sir Thomas was left a widower with two sons. He now turned his attention to field sports, and there is evidence that he did so with great enthusiasm. Two silver goblets of this date are inscribed 'Success to ye Merry Harriers' and 'Prosperity to Fox Hunting'. A notebook also mentions cockfighting, but stag hunting took pride of place. There was no lack of opportunity for this on the Somerset estates. The 'Forest of Exmoor' (an area of about 50 square miles centred on Simonbath) was Crown property, and red deer had been hunted there since the

days of the Conqueror. It was held on lease by a warden, who
was usually the Master of Staghounds as well, and Lady
Acland's uncle, Edward Dyke of Pixton, had occupied both
positions. At his death in 1746 Sir Thomas stepped into his
shoes, and hunted the pack with great energy from one end
of the moor to the other. The North Devon Staghounds, predecessors of the Devon and Somerset Staghounds, were of a
special breed which later became extinct, larger than modern
hounds and with a capacity for travelling long distances and
working in water which was well adapted to the Exmoor
country. There were kennels at Holnicote and at Jury and
Highercombe, both near Pixton; the hounds could use any of
them according to the direction of the day's run. One of the
great yellow-and-white creatures can be seen in Reynolds's
portrait of Sir Thomas in his blue hunting coat,[1] with its head
on its master's knee. A contemporary landscape shows the
whole pack returning to Holnicote at the end of a day's hunting
with the Master and his huntsman, both in blue coats; sadly,
the coiled hunting horns, which were certainly part of the
picture, have faded out of sight. At the end of the day there
was hospitality at whichever house was convenient, for those
who were in at the death. Here is an account of one day's run
which ended at Pixton:[2]

> Dulverton in Co. Somerset. 4 Sept 1759
>
> Sir
>
> I am ordered by my Master Courtenay Walrond Esq to trouble
> you with this letter, that you may have the pleasure of hearing one
> of our finest stag-hunts that ever happened in this Kingdom. About
> / / o'clock Monday morning my Master with his brother and his
> steward Mr Brutton set out from Bradfield, bravely mounted,
> attended by several servants who had horses. About ten they got to
> the Woods & soon after roused the stag at the head of Iron Mill
> Water, when he took to Stuckeridge Wood & crossed the river Exe
> & from thence to Wenham Wood, from that to Cirbury & then into
> Gilbert Wood & then to Ex-clive & from that to Chilly Bridge,
> where he crossed over to /Breford/ Wood, & after running over
> Exmoor Forest & in the whole more then seventy miles he was
> killed near Lowry Gate: when he appeared to be about ten years old,
> his brow bay and trae angles, having all his rights & seven on one top
> & five on the other, and was to one side fourteen hands high. This
> noble chase being ended, my Master his brother and Mr Brutton with

about 20 gentlemen more waited on Sir Thomas Acland at Pixton where each of them drank the health of the stag in a full quart glass of Claret, placed in the Stag's mouth & after drinking several proper healths they went in good order to their respective beds about 2 o'clock and dined with Sir Thomas the next day on a haunch of the noble creature, and about 50 dishes of the greatest rarities among which were several black grouse.

Master, his brother and Mr Brutton rode extremely bold and was in at the death of the Stag. They set out for Bradfield tomorrow evening, and as Sir Thomas has given Master one haunch which weighs 36 pounds and a quarter, he desires you will dine with him on Thursday at Bradfield. I must now conclude, Sir Thomas having given notice of another stag equally as good as this I have described to you, from Brackeridge Wood, for which place the gentlemen are now setting out & I am Sir your most obedt. humble servant Thos. Rich, Park-keeper to Courtenay Walrond Esq. You are desired to bring with you Mr Brutton the hatter & Mr Deake a doctor of Exeter. You may invite likewise if you please any other friend of yours. There were at this chase more than 500 horse and 1,000 foot.

This remarkable letter was found by a barrister of the Middle Temple in 1759, the year in which it was written, at the bottom of a box which had been sent to him from Exeter, together with some wigs, by his barber, whom he knew to be 'a man well-known in the country for his skill in the field as well as in the shop'. Evidently stag hunting was a sport in which the whole countryside could join.

Open house was kept at Pixton and Holnicote throughout the hunting season, and inventories show that each house was richly equipped with quantities of linen and plate. Pixton was the larger establishment (73 tablecloths in 1759, including eight new ones 'of the largest size'), but each of them had a silver dinner-service of five dozen plates and any number of tankards, cups, bowls, dishes and salvers, used not for ornament but for actual eating and drinking, as the scratches on the plates still testify.

Hospitality on this scale was bound to make Sir Thomas a popular figure in the county, and in January 1767 he was invited to stand for election as member of parliament for Somerset. As had happened in Devon, one of the two sitting members died, and Acland was invited to take his place. No opposition was expected. 'It cannot fail striking you how sure

a game it is & how little likely to be attended with expense',
wrote Lord Poulett, who took the chair at 'a very numerous
Meeting of the Gentlemen, Clergy and Freeholders of the
County of Somerset' at Wells. Acland was reluctant. He had
'long declined all thoughts of being in Parliament', he wrote
in reply. Lord Poulett was pressing: it appeared that there were
'different interests' which only Acland could reconcile: his
'known independence in publick' and 'integrity in private life'
were flatteringly mentioned. Eventually he gave in. Alone
among his friends, Thomas Putt of Combe, Gittisham, was
not delighted. '. . . for Godsake my Dear Sir let me beg you not
to loose sight of your native County of Devon,' he wrote to
Sir Thomas. But polling day at Ilchester saw the expected
result, and the new member took his seat in parliament for
the second time. In February 1768 he cast his vote against the
Land Tax, as his constituents expected (his only known vote),
but when a general election was called in the following autumn
he declined in real earnest to stand again. 'My health', he
wrote to the electors, 'would not permit me to give that diligent
Attendance in Parliament so indispensably necessary to the due
discharge of the important Trust reposed in me . . . my Zeal
for the public Service and Welfare of my Country oblige me
therefore to decline all thoughts of any future Parliamentary
engagements.' He certainly had gout at this time, as an entry
in his notebook ('Paid for Gouty Stocking 4s.') shows, but it
seems likely that disinclination also played a part in his refusal.
He was no lover of parliament. Namier and Brooks' comment,
in their *History of the House of Commons,* is 'Twice returned
as a stop-gap'. It sums up Acland's political career.

At 46 Acland was an established landowner in Somerset as
well as in Devon, with a wide circle of influential friends in both
counties, and his loyalties were divided between the two. Tom
Putt's fear was not without foundation. The whole of the
hunting season was spent at Pixton or Holnicote: it is hard
to believe that his favourite country was any other than
Exmoor. He still had obligations to his constituents which
occasionally took him to London, as when, in 1769, he was
sent to present a petition to the king in favour of freeholders'
election rights. However, in the next few years events combined

to turn his attention increasingly in the direction of 'his native county'.

In 1770 his eldest son, John, having come of age and made the Grand Tour, married Lady Harriet Fox-Strangways, daughter of the first Earl of Ilchester. Sir Thomas settled Pixton, Tetton and Petherton Park on the couple, leaving himself Holnicote as his sole hunting-house. At this juncture, even more property came into his possession. In the time of the Civil War a daughter of the first Acland baronet had married into the equally royalist family of Arundell of Trerice. The sole heir of the Arundell estates was at this time William Wentworth and (subject to several lives) he devised them entirely to Sir Thomas Acland, who found himself in possession of substantial amounts of land at Bude and Trerice, near Gunnislake in Cornwall, and also the manors of Selworthy and Luccombe (both additions to Holnicote). By this time Acland property was now at its maximum, and perhaps it was at this period that a legend began to the effect that Sir Thomas could walk from the Bristol Channel to the English Channel without going off his own land. It was never more than a legend, but it was nearer the truth in the late eighteenth century than at any other time.

It was now (with no Pixton for hunting) that Acland began to take more part in the life of Devon. He became a deputy lieutenant in 1773 (being already a justice of the peace), and at about the same time found a new interest in horse-racing. 'The Exeter Races at Hall Down', as *Trewman's Flying Post,* the local paper, described the Haldon races, had not long been established, and attracted great attention every summer. The meetings were social occasions for the whole county: 'The Company was each day very brilliant,' said the *Flying Post* in July 1770, 'and the Town scarce ever known so full . . . last night there was a public Ball at the Hotel which was remarkably splendid.' The culminating event was 'The Great Sweepstakes for the Subscription Cup', this being a splendid two-handled silver-gilt cup with a cover, paid for by 'forty subscribers at ten guineas each', and awarded outright to the winner of the race. Sir Thomas kept race-horses and entered them for this event from 1772 onwards, in competition with his friends, Sir Richard Bampfylde, Sir George Yonge, and—best sportsman of all—John Parker of Saltram. In 1773 his horse came third; then on 6 July 1774 came the moment of triumph, and the *Flying Post* was able to report, 'This day the Sweepstakes was won by Sir Thomas Acland's horse Grecian!' The magnificent trophy, with the horse's name inscribed on a shield, and the steward's name (Francis Rose Drewe) around the rim is still a family heirloom. To Sir Thomas it must have represented the very acme of success. The peak of prosperity had been attained.

In 1775 he gave up the North Devon Staghounds, after nearly thirty years as their Master, and handed them over to Major Bassett. It was probably on this occasion that his many hunting friends combined to present him with a great porcelain jug and punch-bowl and a dozen glasses, all bearing the hunt motto, 'Success to Stag Hunting'. The jug and bowl were specially painted in China from engravings of hunting scenes sent out from England—scenes which must have been quite incomprehensible to the Chinese, and it is hardly surprising that the riders, horses and hounds all have an Oriental character, or that the stag should appear to be half the size of a hound. This in no way spoils the beauty of this lovely family treasure which, to the present time, has remained intact and quite unharmed by the many boisterous toasts which it must have supplied to triumphant stag-hunters.

Acland's attention now turned towards Killerton. A survey drawn in 1756 shows an H-shaped building with a formally laid-out garden and orchard. Agricultural land comes close to the front of the house; of a park there is no sign. This was the Killerton which Thomas Acland had known as a boy, and it was beginning to seem old-fashioned by comparison with the classical mansions, surrounded by large parks, which were making their appearance at Bicton, Castle Hill, and other 'gentlemen's seats' in the county. In particular he must have been struck by the wonderful house at Saltram, recently built for John Parker, and surrounded by beautifully-designed parkland. It may have been in emulation of his friend that he decided to rebuild on his own account. Killerton's greatest asset was its situation, and Sir Thomas decided that the first step must be to 'lay out a park'. He sent for a young man called John Veitch. Veitch was born in 1752, the son of an Edinburgh

nurseryman from whom he received his early training. He had
come south to make his fortune (by popular tradition, travelling
barefoot) and when Acland found him he was 19 years old and
working in London. It is recorded by his descendants that, even
at that age, he 'had some skill in laying out Parks etc. and a
considerable knowledge of forestry': this must have been his
recommendation to Sir Thomas, who now offered him a splendid opportunity to use this skill. It was the beginning of a long
and happy association between the names of Veitch and Acland.

The choice of an architect proved more difficult. In 1775
James Wyatt was commissioned to design a new house, but
there were difficulties and hesitations in the architect-client
relationship. By June 1776 Acland's lawyer was writing from
London suggesting that he should call on Mr. Wyatt 'to press
him for the favour in waiving the Contract'. If Wyatt agreed,
he must have prepared a fresh design, for on 14 April 1778 a
set of drawings showing a palatial building in the Palladian
style was signed by him 'according to my agreement entered
into this day with Sir Thomas Acland'. Probably intended for
a prominent position on top of the hill, Wyatt's new Killerton
never got beyond the drawing-board. Whether Sir Thomas drew
back at the last moment from an enterprise which he felt to be
too grand and too expensive, or whether he merely intended to
postpone it, a different and much more modest scheme was
starting on the ground by the summer of the same year. The
new architect was John Johnson, a Leicestershire man (later
well known as county surveyor for Essex), who was working
on London property development when Acland commissioned
him. He had designed a number of country houses in the
Neo-Classical style, and was recommended by one client as
being 'exceedingly cheap and ingenious'—qualities which may
well have been a strong recommendation to Sir Thomas,
expecially if (as Veitch stated 15 years later, when he was
appealing for repairs to be done to the roof) Killerton 'was
only proposed to stand a few years, during the Building of a
very large House then projected upon the top of the Hill'
(possibly to Wyatt's design). Johnson was very quick and
business-like, and got on so well with his work that by July
1778 Mr. Spring, the builder, was on site taking measurements.

As the new house, temporary or not, was to be more or less in the same position as the old, some of the existing foundations could be used again, and there was a further supply of bricks and stone from 'walls up on the hill', perhaps the remains of an earlier building. Spring's own son drew out any extra plans which were needed ('Offices, Main Drain & etc.') and kept the accounts: the architect wisely kept away. Up to 30 men were employed and paid weekly, and there were also special craftsmen (Johnstone and Robinson, masons; Greenwood, plasterer; Stone, wood-carver), who rendered separate accounts. Progress was excellent. By October the plasterers were at work, by November the 'three Mahogany Doors' had gone up in the Great Parlour, and in April Mr. Spring was writing to Sir Thomas reporting that 'the Carpenters have finished the Chamber Floor above stairs and are now putting in the skylights in the passage . . . finishing the Great Parlour below'. Next month he was begging his client not to 'send the Paper Hangers down before all the rest of the work is compleated'. The house was ready by June 1779, and the builders were about to begin on the stable block, with stone brought down from the remains on the hill. By the beginning of 1780 the stables were complete, and a new turret clock was striking the hour from its cupola.

None of Johnson's drawings has survived, and his original design has been much obscured by later alterations and additions. It was for a simple rectangular two-storey house of pleasant proportions, with plastered walls, a flat roof and parapet, and a good pedimented 'frontispiece', or entrance door, on the south side. A wide arched corridor ran right to the back of the house from this entrance and gave access to the four main rooms. The Great Parlour was enriched with columns and there were decorative plaster friezes, but the ceilings were all plain. Whether it was meant for permanence or not, it was by Sir Thomas's standards a modest house (Plate VIII b).

There was no doubt, however, about the scale and permanence of the new park, and this was the work of young Veitch. Killerton's great charm lay in the contrast between the peaceful slope of the land in front of the house and the volcanic upthrust of the hill behind ('Killerton Clump' or 'Dolbury Hill'), from which, in the words of a nineteenth-century guidebook, there was 'an almost unbounded prospect of richness and fertility'. Veitch fully appreciated this fact. He concentrated on enhancing the landscape as he found it, without trying to impose a pattern of his own, and planted trees so as to emphasise the height of the Clump and frame the views of the country below. About 500 acres were enclosed to form the new park. It was sharply defined by the River Culm on the north and west, and melted imperceptibly into the landscape on the south. To the east, the Exeter-Tiverton road, which came too close to the house, was diverted to set it further away. The fashion of the time demanded interesting objects in the view: the need was met in one direction by the tower of Broadclyst church, while a new octagonal 'Folly' tower filled the gap looking towards Columb John. A herd of fallow deer completed the picture. Alas! the deer and the Folly have gone, but (unlike the house) the park in general remains much as it was when it was first planned (Plate VIII b).

Sir Thomas was 56 when Killerton was finished, still in good health and spirits (there had been another success at the Great Sweepstakes in 1777), and might reasonably have expected some happy years. In fact, they turned out to be tragic ones. His eldest son, John, whose adventures in the American War fill a separate chapter, had only been back in England for a short time when he died in November 1778 at the age of thirty-four. His father's plans for a new house and park must have been with John in mind, and all his hopes were shattered by the tragedy: the heir was a little grandson of a few months old, whom he could never expect to see grow up. There was no more mention of 'a very large house upon the top of the hill' or of Wyatt's grandiose design. That was shelved for ever. Another blow soon fell. The *Flying Post* reported that 'on February 23rd /1779/ Holnicote was burned down in a dreadful fire which entirely consumed the same, with furniture & etc.' Sir Thomas was on the spot. Next morning he was among the ruins, counting the losses and with his own pen checking the lists of silver. Fortunately the precious Exeter Cup was safe, but much else had melted in the fire. He is supposed to have declared that 'he minded the destruction of his valuables less bitterly than the loss of his fine collection of stags' heads', and the remark sounds completely in character. His heart was still in stag-hunting.

John had died leaving a string of debts, and the affairs of his widow and children took up a great deal of Sir Thomas's attention at this time: they continued to live at Pixton and there were numerous money difficulties. Some sales of the Pixton silver had to be arranged. There was much correspondence with the lawyers in these last years of Sir Thomas's life, and they must have been full of worry and disappointment. He made a last attempt at stag-hunting in August 1784, when he returned as co-Master with Major Bassett, 'bringing in some large hounds from Windsor and Stourhead'. But he did not see the season out. On 24 February 1785 he died, at the age of 63, mercifully unaware that his little grandson would only survive him for two months more.

'Little Sir John', the seven-year-old baronet, died on 23 April 1785, and the title passed to his uncle, Thomas, old Sir Thomas's second son. According to tradition he was estranged from his father and living far from home, and had come riding back for a chance visit when he found that his nephew had died and that he himself was the 9th Baronet. The basis for the legend probably lies in his known propensity for getting into debt, and his father's consequent distrust: he had certainly managed to get through the whole of the £10,000 settled on him at the time of his brother's marriage, and old Sir Thomas had felt compelled to make a will in 1784 allowing him only an annuity of £100 and a lump sum of £700 'to settle his debts'. In no circumstances was he to have any access to capital: all was left in trust for his descendants. He shared all his father's tastes, and the two Sir Thomas Dyke Aclands (each was known as 'Sir Thomas his Honour') have frequently been confused in the accounts of Exmoor stag-hunting. Both were Masters of Hounds and valiant in the field, as well as being immensely hospitable to their friends. But, unlike his father, young Sir Thomas had to manage on very slender means, and it is hardly surprising that after his death a great part of Petherton Park estate had to be sold by the trustees to pay his debts. Hunting seems to have been the whole of his life (something which could not fairly be said about his father), and he chose to live only at Holnicote or Highercombe, the family hunting- and shooting-box near Dulverton. Killerton was left to look after itself, with the help of John Veitch, now the agent.

In one respect old Sir Thomas might have envied his son, for in July 1785, only three months after inheriting the title, he married a wife who provided him with a partner for the whole of his life, and long outlived him, to bring up his children in happy security. Henrietta Hoare, the only daughter of Sir Richard Hoare, 1st Baronet of Barn Elms, was a woman who made a lasting mark on the family character. Her own background (of wealth derived from banking) probably added stability to her husband's financial position, and her strong and firm personality contributed qualities which he may himself have lacked. It was a good marriage, though young Sir Thomas only lived nine years to enjoy it, and during this time two sons and two daughters were born. In the same period, as Master of Staghounds (an office which he took over as soon as he could), he killed 101 stags. A collection of their heads is still to be seen in the stables at Holnicote, some with sawn-off antlers, thanks to a groom who found them awkward when he was throwing in hay, and who took the remedy into his own hands.

There are very few records of young Sir Thomas's private life, for after his death his disconsolate widow set about 'destroying all Letters and Papers', but vivid sketches of his hunting days can be found in the diaries of Parson Boyse, the sporting incumbent of Withypool, who followed the hounds keenly and seldom missed a day's run:

1785   Sir Thomas Acland took the command this Spring and killed two Hinds at Porlock.

1789   August 31st . . . Sir Thomas not out—dislocated his shoulder. Autumn Hind Hunting. Holnicote . . . The Hounds kill'd several Sheep. Sir Thomas *ordered* the Huntsman to *Hang Himself* and the whole Pack.
        August 21st. Holnicote. He /the stag/ was seen standing in Yelcombe in Horner /then Cloutsham, Stoke Pero, Blackford/ up to Alderman's Barrow. Here Sir. Thos.'s Horse (Highover) fell with him and lamed himself. /Stag finally killed at Lifford Bridge . . . miles from Horner, nr Cheriton/ Sir Thomas Ran from Cheriton and was in at the Death. Highover gave up.

1790   Previous to Stag-hunting July 5th. Found a Hind and a Stag
        in Horner . . . a most excellent run /finished up at Napstock:
        huntsman's horse 'completely done' at Exford and 'lodged
        there the night'/ Sir Thomas was at the Death.

1791   Oct. 22. Sir Thomas was taken very ill and went to London.

There is no record of what this illness was, but it was enough
to keep him off the hunting field, for there is no mention of his
name in this or the following season. In 1793 he reappears:

Stag-Hunting 1793. Dulverton Sept 6. Found in Mountsey
Castle. Killed under Heighley Wear. Very remarkable for a
short body. Uncommonly fat . . . the Hounds killed several
sheep. Sir Thomas in the Horrors.

1793   Holnicote. Sept 12th. Found in Withycombe. Killed at Porlock
        Wear. A good Stag and a fine chase. Sir Thos's Horse (Chance)
        dead tired.

The last mention of Sir Thomas in Parson Boyse's diary is
heavily underlined, as if in mourning:

Memorandum. Sir Thomas Acland Died on the 17th day of May 1794

Apparently he was taken ill unexpectedly on another journey
to London, and this time did not recover. His family and friends
were deeply shocked. He was buried in the family vault at
Broadclyst, by his cousin John Acland the vicar, but it is in
the burial register of Selworthy, parish church of his beloved
Holnicote, that his epitaph is written:

Hic finis fatorum Priami hic exitus illum
Sorte tulit!—Vale. Vale. Vale.
Neo Meridies nec Aurora unquam vident ejus ora.
Reliquit nobis cornu, canes, tandem quiescant ejus manes.

This was the fated end of Priam's empire and of his own life!
—Farewell. Farewell. Farewell. Neither noon nor Dawn shall
ever see his face again. He left us his horn and his hounds;
may his spirit finally rest in peace!

It was indeed farewell. The horns and the hounds remained,
but the human ghosts were silent. The sporting squires had
had their day.

Chapter Four

THE AMERICAN ADVENTURE (1770–1778)

AFTER SIR THOMAS'S death his last stag's head was hung at Pixton, where he and his father had drunk so many toasts to sport. This house, as well as Tetton, belonged to his widowed sister-in-law, Lady Harriet Acland, who had long ago resigned herself to the fact that she had no son to inherit the family title which had now gone to her little nephew, Tom. For most people the recent horrors of the French Revolution had blotted out the memory of the American War of Independence, in which Harriet had played so brave a part 17 years ago, but for her the remembrance was as fresh as ever. She seldom spoke much about it; but when she did so her listeners were always struck by the contrast between her gentle appearance and the enormous strength of character which her story revealed. As a contemporary engraving records, 'This amiable Lady accompanied her husband to Canada in the Year 1776, & during two campaigns under went such fatigue and distress as female fortitude was thought incapable of supporting.'

John and Harriet were married in 1770 when Acland prosperity was near its peak. John had all his father's energy and a fiery temper besides: on returning from the Grand Tour he had picked such a quarrel with his boon companion that both young men refused to own a joint portrait, especially commissioned from Reynolds to commemorate their eternal friendship. The same impetuosity marked the whole of John's career. Harriet's relations were aristocratic and Whig—she was second cousin to Charles James Fox, and moved in the circle which gathered at Holland House—and they considered that her husband was something of a provincial boor with old-fashioned Tory opinions.

Political feeling in London was running very high at this time on account of George III's determination to govern the country himself through a Tory majority mainly made up of his own 'King's Friends' and ambitious place-hunters under the compliant premiership of Lord North; a state of affairs which, to Whigs like Burke and Fox, was the very negation of parliamentary democracy. The issue was brought to a head by the American colonists' resentment of 'taxation without representation' and their subsequent resolve to achieve political independence. The king held implacable views on the subject, and hot debates filled every coffee-house and gentleman's club in London. Political argument was very much to John Acland's taste, and although he boasted of being a simple country squire 'not blessed with those abilities which teach us to understand black when we read white', he was in reality a fluent and effective speaker. In 1774 he entered parliament as Tory member for Callington in Cornwall—a mere matter of bribing the four dozen electors and keeping open house at the *New Inn*— and from the moment when he rose to his feet in the House of Commons there was no doubt about his political sympathies. By this time the American troubles were approaching flashpoint, and opinion was divided between those who wanted to bring the colonists firmly to heel and those who believed that further concessions would bring peace. To John Acland the question was quite clear, and he poured scorn on some half-hearted conciliatory proposals of Lord North, denouncing them in a stream of warm eloquence as 'nugatory and humiliating' and certain to result in 'a total convulsion of the British Empire' and 'utter ruin' if proceeded with. Even George III was somewhat alarmed when he read the speech next morning, and he confided to his prime minister that it might be better to discourage this spirited young supporter from following a military career.

John was not to be discouraged. He was already an enthusiastic colonel of Militia in Devon, and he now became a regular soldier as well by buying himself a commission in an infantry regiment; when he next spoke in the House it was as a military man. In April the American situation changed dramatically, with the shots fired at Lexington and Concord, and King

George, when he opened the new session of parliament in October, spoke frankly of a 'rebellious War'. John was awarded the privilege of moving the formal vote of thanks in the Commons, and he did so in terms which his opponents described as 'fulsome and adulatory': he was a particular target for Whig criticism on account of an address which, as colonel of the 1st Battalion of the Devon Militia, he had recently presented to the king in person without going through parliament. Framed in John's usual intemperate style, the 'Loyal Address' pledged aid to the monarch whenever and wherever called upon to put down sedition, and it spoke of His Majesty's Opposition as if its members were rebels like the Americans. It was a dangerous mistake—also made at this time by other bodies of Militia—which threatened to link the armed forces with party politics in a way which Britain had determined should never happen, and John received savage treatment in the Commons. Fox supposed that the Devonshire Militia wanted to 'alienate the King from the people, to imbrue their hands in the blood of their fellow-subjects: such men, he thought, ought not to be trusted with arms'. John was not in the least deterred. He had many friends in the army, one of whom was General Burgoyne, and when Burgoyne was ordered across the Atlantic, at the head of an army, to reinforce the British troops in Canada, he took John Acland with him as a Major of Grenadiers in the 20th Foot.

Harriet now showed her true mettle and proved to her relations that they had no need to pity her for her rough husband. Never was there a more devoted wife. This young and gently-nurtured girl in her twenties, a popular figure in London society, where she was considered 'vastly pretty', decided to go with Major Acland wherever he went, and leaving her two infant daughters with her mother in Dorset, she travelled to Ireland where John was waiting to sail. He begged her not to come, but hers was the stronger will, and she got her way. So began Harriet's American adventure.

On 8 April 1776 the great fleet of 42 transport ships sailed out of Cork harbour with six regiments on board, to be joined within a few days by a second flotilla carrying German mercenaries from Brunswick. The Aclands were in the *Kent,* a

square-rigged East Indiaman large enough to hold five companies
of the 20th Foot—about 250 men and 15 officers. Some of the
soldiers were allowed to take their wives and children (there
was a cow on board to provide milk), but Harriet was the only
officer's lady. Before the vessel was a week out of Cork, a
strong gale overturned her bureau and broke much glass and
china, and next day the swell was so heavy that she could not
see the top-gallant mast-heads of ships a quarter of a mile
away; but if she was ill she never recorded it in her journal,
merely observing that some of the soldiers were very sick. The
sea-voyage took six weeks. In was 28 April ('as cold as at Pixton
in December') when Jack Ketch, the Aclands' dog, smelled
land, and 23 May before the two fleets assembled in the Gulf of
St. Lawrence and waited for pilots from Quebec to guide them
up the river. A few days later a little party from the *Kent*
landed for a picnic—'the first American ground we ever stept
on: it is easy to conceive how happy we were once more to feel
terra firma under us, many of us having never been 3 days
together at sea before', wrote Harriet, who felt that she was
'walking on magic ground' among the forest trees of Labrador.

On 27 May the fleets came to anchor in the basin at Quebec.
Here Governor-General Carleton had his headquarters. For most
of the winter he had been struggling, with very limited resources,
to avert an American invasion of Canada. He had succeeded in
fighting the rebels away from Quebec, but they were in possession of Montreal, 120 miles further up the St. Lawrence. This
city was in a most strategically important position, for it stood
at the head of a long chain of lakes and rivers which ran straight
down to the Hudson and New York. Two forts of special importance, at Crown Point and Ticonderoga, about a third of the
way down the 400-mile-long natural waterway, separating the
two great lakes of George and Champlain, had been in rebel
hands since the previous summer. General Carleton's great
object was to flush the Americans out of Montreal and chase
them down Lake Champlain to the forts as the preliminary to
a full-scale invasion of the colonies, and with Burgoyne's
reinforcements the first objective was soon achieved, but to go
further needed boats as well as men, and it was 3 October
before a fleet was ready. In that bitter climate only five or

six weeks more of fighting weather remained and, although Carleton reached the end of the lake and took Crown Point, he was forced to leave the more distant fort of Ticonderoga unconquered and return to winter quarters in Montreal.

Harriet meanwhile had stayed behind, with a brief and characteristically intrepid excursion by sledge to nurse John through an illness in a remote outpost. The two now spent a comfortable winter with the other officers until the ice thawed again on the St. Lawrence, when Burgoyne appeared back from an expedition to London with new orders. He was himself to lead a specially-picked force two-thirds of the way down the Champlain–George–Hudson waterway as far as Albany, where he would be met by one British army coming up from New York and another from the west. The American colonies would then be hopelessly divided, and Burgoyne—who had staked his whole reputation on the success of the enterprise—believed that the war would be ended. Over-ambition was to be his undoing.

'Gentleman Johnny' Burgoyne's army of 10,000 men, which set out from Montreal on 10 June 1777, included British and German troops, and a considerable body of Indians ('savages' as Harriet called them, having seen the recruiting ceremony with hatchets and war-whoops: 'a curious but a very horrible and disagreeable sight'). Of course she was keen to go with her husband, but he forbade it, and she remained in Montreal, presenting him and all the other officers with half a Cheshire cheese apiece to augment their rations. However, when she heard in July that Ticonderoga was taken and Major Acland wounded, nothing would stop her from commandeering a boat and going down Lake Champlain to nurse him. When he recovered he had no heart to bully her any further. A carriage was hastily improvised, and in this Harriet travelled down the Hudson valley at the rear of the army, insisting on going forward every night to share her husband's tent, which was always in the most advanced position, because he commanded the Grenadiers. There were unpleasant sounds: shots, howling wolves, and—most horrible of all to Harriet—the Indians' 'dead yells' which signified the number of enemy stragglers caught in the woods and probably scalped. Nevertheless, she remained stoical throughout, even when Jack Ketch upset a lighted candle in the tent and nearly burnt his master and mistress alive.

By the end of August Burgoyne had reached a point near enough to Albany for him to halt his army on the east side of the Hudson and wait for the promised reinforcements, but even by 13 September they had not arrived. Supplies were running low and the season was well advanced. There was still plenty of time for the army to retrace its steps to Montreal as some of Burgoyne's officers advised, but his vanity drove him on. Perhaps he had always secretly hoped that the victory would be his and his alone. At any rate, he ignored all advice and, constructing a pontoon bridge, crossed the river and took up a position in Saratoga. It was a fatal move, which cost him his reputation as a general. His supply lines on the opposite bank were immediately cut by the Americans, and an unexpectedly large enemy force under the command of General Gates stood prepared to block his way to Albany. The British reinforcements never came.

The two battles of Saratoga now followed with an interval of 18 days between them. Burgoyne led the attack on both occasions. The first resulted in heavy British losses, but led to no conclusive result. The second, on 7 October, was the desperate attempt of a starving army and it ended in total defeat. Major Acland, who ordered his Grenadiers to 'fix bayonets and charge the damned Rebels' was one of the first to fall, wounded by rifle bullets through both legs. So quickly did the Americans rush past that John's men had no chance of rescuing him, and he was left on the field as a prisoner.

Harriet knew nothing about it until the evening. She shared a farm building with three other officers' wives, one of them the German Baroness Riedesel, and here an extraordinary semblance of domestic life went on, even when the army surgeons were forced to use the building as a field hospital. When General Fraser was brought in dying, the Baroness had to clear the dinner-table for him to lie on, and hurry her three children into another room; he died, apologising to her for his groans. One of the other officers' wives was made a widow during the evening, and the other saw her husband brought in badly wounded. When Harriet heard the news of John her anxiety

must have been appalling; yet the effect on this truly remarkable woman was merely to screw her courage to its highest
pitch. She approached Burgoyne, who was preparing for a
dejected retreat, and to his horrified amazement begged him
to let her cross the enemy lines to nurse her husband. It could
only be done safely by water and at night. With the greatest
possible reluctance he scribbled a *laissez-passer* to Gates, begging
in sycophantic terms for special treatment on account of
Harriet's rank, pressed the 'wet dirty bit of paper' into her
hand and let her go off down the river in an open boat with
two servants and a chaplain, who bore a flag of truce. It was
10 o'clock at night in October, and raining hard. Harriet was
several months pregnant. Nevertheless, she conducted herself
with her usual coolness until the first enemy sentry was reached,
two miles downstream. Contrary to a biased account, which
Burgoyne wrote to justify his collapse, the British party was
taken on shore with the least possible delay and Harriet was
made comfortable in the guard-house while Major Dearborn,
the officer on guard, took her note to his superiors, Enoch Poor
and Horatio Gates. Gates was very much annoyed that Burgoyne
should beg, as a special favour, what he himself regarded as
ordinary decent conduct, and he wrote back angrily, saying that
he always treated his prisoners with humanity.

On 14 October Burgoyne formally surrendered his army to
Gates, and the defeat encouraged the French to come to
America's aid. When Gentleman Johnny returned to England,
in exchange for enemy prisoners, he found himself in disgrace
with the government, and was required to give an account of
his whole expedition. The Whigs thought that he had lost the
war by crossing the Hudson river, and they proved to be right.

Dislike between the two sides had much increased during
Burgoyne's campaign, partly on account of his use of mercen-
aries and Indians: as the Earl of Chatham said in the House of
Lords, during a debate on the battle of Saratoga, 'the German
Bayonet and the Indian Scalping-knife were much resented'.
It is pleasant to record that John and Harriet Acland did
something, however small, to restore mutual respect. The
American army went into winter quarters at Albany, where
Harriet nursed her husband for nine weeks before he could

get out of bed, and during that time they had most cordial relations with General Gates and his officers. Gates had been born and educated in England, and had served in the British army; it was natural for him to write to his wife Betsy about John as 'old Sir Thomas's son' as if they had known each other in old days. He added that the major was a 'most confounded Tory' whom he hoped to make into as good a Whig as himself, and described Harriet tenderly as 'a delicate piece of quality'. (Dearborn and Poor must also have been friendly, for nearly a century later John's great-great-nephew Charles recorded that on a visit to America he was 'twice warmly greeted by Captain Dearborn and Mr. Poor, librarian at Washington, because their names were connected with that of Colonel Acland'.) The Aclands parted almost with regret from their new friends, John having considerably revised his opinion of the 'Rebels'. As soon as he was well enough to travel, Gates allowed him to return to England with his party, on the understanding that exchange prisoners would be sent back, and Harriet arrived home in time for the birth of her baby son in February 1778.

The Aclands now found themselves celebrities on account of Harriet's exploit, which was seen as one of the few bright events in a dismal campaign. An imaginary picture of the scene on the Hudson (Plate IX) was hung in the Royal Academy and later made the subject of a widely-published engraving which included Burgoyne's account. George III sent for Major Acland as a brave man who was likely to give a sound account of the battle, and encouraged him to resume his seat in the Commons. However, John did not speak again. Even if Gates had not made him into a Whig, his opinion of the Americans and their treatment of prisoners was warmer than would have been expected of a Tory, and if he argued on the subject he did so in private. A legend grew up after his premature death in November that he had died fighting a duel with a fellow officer of Militia who had disparaged the Rebels, but an account of the duel itself, written by John's second, shows that the cause was trifling—a complaint about a dinner invitation and a fancied insult from a junior officer—and that no effective shot was fired. Perhaps John's quick temper was to blame. He rode back to Pixton unharmed, but the chill damp of a November dawn finished the work which the American bullets had begun, and this time Harriet could not help him. He died on 15 November 1778 at the age of 34, leaving a widow who was to mourn him for 37 years.

Harriet's hopes now centred on her son, John, and it was the second—and perhaps the greatest—sorrow of her life when the little boy died at seven years old, a few weeks after inheriting the title from his grandfather. She continued to live at Pixton until her one remaining child, Elizabeth Kitty, married the 2nd Earl of Carnarvon in 1796, taking with her as dowry the Pixton and Tetton estates, together with a considerable amount of personal property. Harriet then went to Tetton as dowager, and lived there until her death in 1815, the year of Waterloo. She was a legend in her lifetime, and her courage supported her to the end, for it was eventually revealed that she had suffered terrible pain from cancer for years without complaining. The title had long since gone to her nephew, Tom, whom she had seen grow up, marry, and enter parliament before she died, and he played his part with distinction; yet Aclands must always regret that they cannot claim direct descent from this most gallant member of the family, but the American adventure was over for good.[1]

Chapter Five

A NEW FAMILY PATTERN (1787-1808)

TOM WAS SEVEN when his father died, 'a little ruddy black-headed boy', eldest of the five brothers and sisters who grew up together at Holnicote to enjoy a country childhood. It was taken for granted that Tom would follow the pattern of the sporting squires. At his birth, toasts were drunk from the celebrated Chinese punch-bowl and jug, 'with oft-repeated hopes that he would become as famous a stag-hunter as his father', and, seven years later, one of his mother's first worries as a widow was to find a way of keeping the Mastership of Hounds for him when he came of age. It would be 'sad work' if the pack went into other hands, she wrote to her brother. Yet events turned out quite differently. By the time Tom was 21 a new century had started, and a more serious climate of opinion was beginning to influence both private and public life. There was no more hunting at Holnicote: instead, politics and philanthropy absorbed the energy and enthusiasm which he had inherited from his forebears. 'The Great Sir Thomas', as his descendants affectionately call him, earned the title not by feats of sportsmanship and hospitality, but by public work and the patriarchal rule of a large family and wide estates; his long reign embraced the climax of the Victorian age and, though no stereotype, he typified it just as much as his father and grandfather had typified the eighteenth century.

William Owen painted him as a young member of parliament standing by the hustings on Exeter Castle and towering, more than life-size, over the Devon landscape—the very embodiment of earnest vigour (Plate X). In much the same way he towers over the family chronicle. Certain qualities, which may or may not have been latent in his ancestors, combined in his character to form a new pattern: all the vitality and enthusiasm of the sporting squires was still there, but they were fused with a fresh sense of moral and social purpose. Money previously lavished on stag-hunting and good living was now to be spent on estate improvements, political elections, and the furtherance of good causes. To serve in parliament was no mere duty, as it had been for his grandfather, but a welcome opportunity to further his ideals. Acland had a singular independence of thought and action which he maintained even when it cut across his own interests. Other people's good opinion was of no account to him. If his conscience dictated a certain course he followed it, regardless of personal consequences to himself, or of the feelings of his friends. It was a quality which enabled him to see ahead of his time, and to break away from the conventions of his background. In this spirit ('never a quite satisfactory party man'), he deserted his fellow Tories to vote for a vital second reading of the Reform Bill, and supported Catholic Emancipation, to the horror of his Evangelical friends and county neighbours. The same pattern was to repeat itself again and again in future generations.

Young Sir Thomas had a long minority. His money was all in the hands of trustees and guardians until he came of age. His mother, Henrietta, felt an enormous responsibility for bringing him up in the best possible way. She had been devoted to her first husband, but his recklessly open-handed style of living had left the estates with many debts, and she may well have wanted to set a different course for his son and heir. She was expecting her fifth child, and felt distraught at the prospect of looking after her family single-handed, dependent for money on the goodwill of the trustees. She refused to live at Killerton, as they suggested: the very idea of a move made her 'uncomfortable'. Would the trustees allow her enough money if she disagreed with them? 'I give up the point of ever being happy,' she declared. 'It appears I shall never be settled more.' However, being a masterful woman with the common sense of her banking ancestors, she carried her point with the trustees, and continued to live at Holnicote, leaving Killerton empty until Tom should come of age. Moreover, within a bare year of widowhood, she was happily re-married to Captain Matthew

Fortescue, R.N. (brother of the first Earl Fortescue of Castle Hill in North Devon, one of Tom's guardians), and soon presented him with two more sons to add to the already large family. She could now fairly count herself as 'settled'.

Captain Fortescue provided support which was essential to Henrietta's happiness, but it was her personality, rather than his, which dominated the children's unbringing. Tom was her prime concern. She was determined that he should grow up 'well fitted to take his proper place in the world'. He must have sound religious principles, be punctual and diligent, avoid debt and drink, and 'cultivate an outward manner fit for any society'. How to achieve this, with a high-spirited boy who knew that he would inherit a large fortune, was a puzzle. As a first step, he was sent away to a private school in north London (the first 'eight-year-old baronet in his own right' ever to be seen there), and at 14, on the advice of his guardians, he went to Harrow. His mother who, with reason, believed that the public schools of the day were 'not conducive to good manners' would have preferred to keep him at home with tutors, but she was over-ruled. There was comfort in the fact that the new rector of Selworthy, 30-year-old Joshua Stephenson, seemed certain to be a good influence. He had been presented to the family living with the idea of keeping it warm for a younger son, but Tom, at 15, found him a congenial companion, and was soon begging him to stay permanently. Stephenson readily agreed, and soon became as much a family chaplain as a parish priest. His quiet churchmanship, typical of the eighteenth, rather than the nineteenth, century, was undisturbed by the 'enthusiasm' of the Evangelicals (or, later, by the Tractarians), and he maintained a steadying influence on the younger man throughout his life. Acland repaid him with an unswerving respect and affection which continued during the whole 60 years of the rector's incumbency.

When she was not busy with the welfare of her seven children (Charles and Hugh Acland were packed off into the Navy, William and Henry Fortescue to public schools), Henrietta looked after Holnicote estate, doctored the poor of the parish and, with her husband, Matthew, became an enthusiastic painter, learning to sketch from the artist, Francis Nicholson, who often came to stay at Holnicote. Both pupils became adept, and large landscapes began to fill the house. Tom and his brothers also learned to draw, and in later life used their talents to advantage. Henrietta's views on religion were firm. She did not like the Evangelicals, and said so to her son. She considered that they 'had a particular starch look', which marked them the moment they came into a room. Worse still, Hannah More, a priestess of the group known as the extremely Evangelical Clapham Sect, had 'a scrutinizing artful countenance' and was 'rather vulgar' in manner. She made Henrietta feel a heathen, so that it is remarkable that she smiled so readily on Tom's choice of Lydia Hoare (a third cousin) as his future wife, knowing that Lydia's brother, William, lived on Clapham Common, and that her father, Henry Hoare, though not himself a member of the Sect, was friendly with William Wilberforce, Henry Thornton, Hannah More, and other members. Luckily, however, Mr. Hoare, who was head partner in the family bank and rode up to Fleet Street every day from his house at Mitcham in Surrey, was not an 'enthusiast'. When Miss More came on a visit, he regarded her with awe, but was not in agreement with her strict opinions. Unlike 'holy Hannah', he and his wife did not consider it wrong to sing, play the piano, or go to the theatre, and Lydia was brought up to enjoy all these things with grace. She first came to Holnicote with her parents in November 1804, when Tom was 17 and just preparing for Oxford. A visitor to the house considered that her appearance 'rather excited respect than love at first sight', but in Tom it seems to have excited both, for it was soon a settled thing that they would marry when he came of age. Henrietta was delighted with her. Lydia was exactly what she had wished for—'natural', modest, accomplished, and, for the present, compliant. There was a little apprehension when Hannah More came over from her home near Bristol to visit her old friends: Mrs. Hoare prevented her daughter from playing the piano, lest this be thought 'trifling'. Henrietta was delighted to find that Lydia joined with herself in silent dislike of the great lady. It set the final seal on her approval.

Tom went up to Oxford in March 1806 and entered Christ Church as a gentleman-commoner. His mother had already exacted a promise that he would drink no wine, and now she pursued him with twice-weekly letters of admonition, scolding him if he did not immediately reply. 'You have been very inattentive to me,' she would write '. . . I was not at all pleased with the one I had yesterday, as one would have thought rather it had been written by a School Boy than by a young man.' She instructed him about his friends (those of 'higher rank and ability' than himself should be sought: Evangelicals must be avoided), his plans (no travelling on Sundays), and his health ('I must *insist* on your not sitting up till five o'clock in the morning'). Between his studies and his love for Lydia poor Tom was a prey to alternate states of exhilaration and depression, but Henrietta did not sympathise. 'As always you go to extremes,' she wrote: 'send for some salts and wash away your nonsense.'

In spite of the hectoring tone, Tom treasured his mother's letters and tied them together with ribbon, though the advice they contained was largely neglected. To the end of his days, he never learned to be punctual, write a clear hand, or manage his money, and he cared as little about cultivating his betters as he did about cold-shouldering the Evangelicals. His character was developing in a direction of its own. He found himself at the centre of a group of friends who, as he wrote in later life, 'lived together in the most cordial intimacy of Christ Church', and in their company his horizons were stretched beyond those of the conventional young squire preparing (in his mother's words), to 'take his place in the County'. The 'Christ Church Debating Society' or 'the Brotherhood', as they called themselves, met regularly for discussion on topics of the day. Most of them became members of parliament, and in due course they formed the nucleus of the well-known Grillion's Club, whose stated aim was to bring together men of differing political opinions. It is certain, therefore, that Tom had his first taste of serious debate at Oxford, and learned there to develop his talent for speaking. Many of the Brotherhood remained his lasting friends, and one in particular, Robert Harry Inglis, who later became a noted politician of High Tory views, became his trusted adviser and confidant for the rest of his life. Letters from Tom's fellow undergraduates show him as a young man full of energy and adventure, and a good friend in time of trouble. Inglis himself, who was known for his moral principles, was helped out of the most embarrassing sort of scrape on the eve of his engagement, and declared thereafter that he needed Tom's moral support in order to walk uprightly. Tom's short time at Oxford ended in June 1807 when he took his final examinations. The results must have been satisfactory, for Inglis wrote enthusiastically of 'a glorious Termination of a glorious Career', and even Henrietta owned that she was pleased.

Tom did not rest for long upon his laurels. After the briefest of visits to Holnicote to say goodbye to his mother and Lydia, he was off on a sketching expedition to Norway. The Napoleonic Wars, which by now had closed most of the Continent, had not succeeded in killing the notion that the best way to finish off a gentleman's education was to travel abroad, and most of Tom's friends meant to do so as soon as peace came. Characteristically, Tom was not prepared to wait, and he picked Scandinavia as a good choice, for Sweden and Denmark-Norway were still neutral (though an attack from Napoleon was always feared), and Norway possessed the finest scenery outside Switzerland for sketching. All the same, there was an obvious risk in going. Reginald Heber, an Oxford friend who had already made the tour, assured Tom that there would be 'no Robbers and but little Cheating', but advised taking a sabre all the same: Lydia was wretched, and her father, Henry Hoare, considered the scheme 'next to madness'. If Napoleon invaded Denmark, what would happen? Tom would be taken prisoner and be unable to return to England for his wedding. Tom heeded neither Lydia's feelings nor Mr. Hoare's advice, and he set out on 17 July with two companions and a servant, prepared for anything. Hardly had they settled down to sketch in Norway when all fears were realised. Canning, the British prime minister, ordered the bombardment of Copenhagen in order to forestall Napoleon, and the Danish fleet was virtually wiped out. Immediately Denmark and her reluctant subject-nation, Norway, found themselves at war with Britain, and naturally enough the travellers were cast into prison in the Norwegian town of Köngsberg. It is a family tradition that

Tom spoke too rashly on this occasion, and was punished for it. If, as seems likely, he was protesting against the sovereignty of Denmark over Norway (which the Norwegians much resented), it may well account for the fact that the Norwegian officials released the prisoners after only two months, and granted them a safe passage home across Sweden. At all events Tom arrived back at Holnicote in January, to the great relief of his family and friends, bringing with him many tales of adventure and a portfolio of sketches, some of which were worked up by Francis Nicholson and exhibited at the Royal Academy. He had made a number of friends with whom he continued to correspond, and he had left behind him a gift of £500 for the relief of sufferers from the war. So ended an adventure which revealed at the very outset of his career all his main characteristics. No doubt the most apparent to casual observers were his impatient energy, reckless love of adventure, and disregard of the feelings and advice of others, but it was more significant that he showed so early the concern for the underdog, the courage to speak freely, even when it put him in danger, and the warm generosity to those in need, which were to be his best qualities throughout life.

If Lydia expected Tom to stay at home for the two months remaining before his coming-of-age, she was disappointed, for after a bare two weeks he disappeared again—this time to Edinburgh, where a group of his Christ Church friends were spending the winter in order to attend the university lectures on moral philosophy and political economy which were earning the city the title of the 'Athens of the North'. This time, however, Lydia's patience was not tested for long. In March Tom came down to London in time for his 21st birthday: there was a dinner party of 23 people to mark the occasion, and Mr. Stephenson came up from Selworthy, and bought a new black suit. On 7 April 1808 Tom and Lydia were married, and started on their 48 years of married partnership.

Chapter Six

THE GREAT SIR THOMAS (1808–1871)

Tom and Lydia

AN ENTIRELY NEW STAGE of life now started for Tom. It was one for which he was very ill-prepared. During his minority all his affairs had been managed by other people—guardians, trustees, bailiffs, the family lawyer and his mother, with very little reference to his own opinions. His income had consisted solely of a slender allowance from the trustees. Now everything was changed. He found himself with an income of £10,000, answerable to no one, and with responsibility for all his estates, which were now even larger than before, thanks to the trustees' prudent management. Except for Holnicote, where he had been brought up, he had very little detailed knowledge of any of them. He and Lydia were to live at Killerton, but he knew hardly anything about it: the house was dilapidated after 30 years of neglect, and needed repairing and refurbishing. He thought it best to stay in London until the summer and leave all the arrangements to his mother and John Veitch (now the agent), who had looked after the place since it was rebuilt and was delighted to see it come alive again. Henrietta, too, was pleased to be in charge of choosing new carpets and curtains. An organ was built for Lydia, superfluous windows were blocked up to avoid the window tax, and a set of elegant furniture was ordered from Carter, the Exeter cabinet-maker ('uncommonly good and much cheaper than Chippendale' as a visitor commented). She also arranged for extensive alterations and repairs at Holnicote, where she and Matthew were to live. The whole bill came to £4,000—'there is one thing for your consolation,' she wrote to her son, 'there can be no repairs wanted to either of your houses for years to come.'

45

Tom was not unduly distressed: he had himself just spent
£56,000 on a considerable amount of land in Broadclyst in
order to round off the Killerton estate, with the intention of
selling another estate at Seaton, recently bought by the trustees.
In vain did his father-in-law and Mr. Weech, the family lawyer,
point out that Seaton was a better investment in view of its
likely development as a watering-place: such considerations
interested Tom very little. 'After my minority,' he wrote to
Weech, 'I do not like to feel myself shackled in any point.'
This remained his attitude throughout life. He never learned
to live within his income and, though this worried him a great
deal whenever he allowed it to rise to the surface of his mind,
it never prevented him from doing anything that he considered
worthwhile, and anything that he wanted to do.

The first task to be tackled was the care of the Acland
estates, and Killerton took precedence. Acland was anxious to
develop the house and its surroundings into something more
elaborate than his grandfather had contemplated, and Lydia,
who herself came from a lovely house and garden at Mitcham,
was just as keen: naturally, John Veitch (by now a respected
landscape consultant and nurseryman in his own right, as well
as agent) was eager to co-operate. They planned an imaginative
scheme for the whole of the garden and park, with much planting to enhance the beauty of the views, and a mile-long sunk
fence to keep the deer under control. The garden, complete
with an underground ice-house, was to be laid out with grass
glades, gravel walks, thickets and 'single Trees . . . to Forrest
[sic] parts of the Lawn for your Amusement for years to
come', wrote Veitch to his new master. With its farms and
cottages, forest, saw-mill, estate yard and stables, Killerton
bristled with problems, and the other estates in Somerset and
Cornwall were no easier to manage. Acland was acutely aware
of his want of detailed knowledge. 'I would thank you to send
me a short Abstract of the present state of my Affairs,' he
wrote to Weech, his solicitor, 'and how I stand in respect of
Rents.' He commissioned a thorough survey and valuation of
all the properties, and made plans to visit them in turn as soon
as he could. Meanwhile, he was extremely concerned about the
state of the poor in Broadclyst. The parish, according to Veitch,

was 'allowed to be good to the poor', largely because the Rev. John Acland, Sir Thomas, the grandfather's first cousin, had been vicar for the 40 years up to 1795, and had pioneered a 'State Friendly Society' which might have anticipated Beveridge, had it become law. An unusually generous amount was paid to the parishioners out of the Poor Rate; nevertheless, 400 people were poor enough to beg for a penny piece from Veitch on Christmas Day, and 100 had to be turned away from the 'birthday beef' which celebrated Sir Thomas's coming-of-age. He was distressed, and suggested that a soup-kitchen should be set up to cater for the needs of the whole parish during the winter; Veitch, however, persuaded him that selective grants of food and clothing would do more good. In the end, it was left between him and the vicar to see what could be done for £100, a comparatively liberal amount at a time when an exceptionally thrifty labourer's live-savings were unlikely to amount to more than twenty pounds.

In September 1808 the Aclands were off again to spend another winter in Edinburgh, pausing for a sketching tour of the Lake District on their way. With so much still to be seen to, it is no wonder that exasperation coloured all the letters from home. 'I shall wish your journey to Scotland farther, or rather nearer, if my head is to have the bother of so many of your affairs,' wrote Henrietta. 'I am bothered half out of my senses with these farms.' Veitch sent long, detailed letters about tenancies, insurance, the stables, the deer, and the progress in the garden and park, many of them needing urgent answers which were slow to come. Weech and Lydia's father tried to explain business matters at a distance, with equally little result. Tom's time in Edinburgh was taken up with lectures on moral philosophy and political economy, and the society of his old Christ Church friends who continued to meet for debates. His absence from home was no mere escape. He was very anxious, as he wrote to his father-in-law, 'to form a Course in Life which a wise Man would not repent and which a Christian would not fear', and he was conscious that he had not as yet achieved it. Although he had inherited his mother's strong sense of duty, he did not share all her religious views, and was not in the least averse to the Evangelicals. His friend,

Robert Inglis, was close to the Clapham Sect, and through him and the Hoare family he began to be intimate with Wilberforce, Henry Thornton, and some of its other members. Unlike Henrietta, he saw much to admire in Hannah More, who with her four sisters made her home at Barley Hill, near Bristol, a centre for those who were interested in religion. Here the Aclands met Alexander Knox, an extraordinarily open-minded and influential Irish theologian, who described himself as a 'Methodist Highchurchman', and who, with his friend, Bishop Jebb, was a forerunner of the Tractarians. In this sort of company, Acland had begun to think for himself and it was for the sake of developing his own philosophy that he spent the second winter of study in Edinburgh. However, with the spring came Lydia's morning-sickness, and it was obvious that they ought to go home.

On 25 May 1809 their eldest child was born at Killerton, and christened after his father, Thomas Dyke Acland. It was the start of 18 years of child-bearing for Lady Acland. During that time 10 children were born—six of them in seven years—yet, thanks to a strong constitution and a large domestic staff which usually included a wet-nurse, she was seldom prevented from joining her husband in what Henrietta termed his 'peregrinations'. For the moment, however, she was able to settle down in peace at Killerton while Acland (as his wife and mother now called him) was fully engaged in establishing his position in the county as sheriff and justice of the peace, and making himself familiar with the details of the estates. Her chief interests, apart from domestic duties, were the garden and music. The little rustic summer-house now called 'The Bear's Hut' was built for her pleasure, and she loved to discuss new plans with Veitch, and to exchange plants with friends. Frequent visits were made between Killerton and Stourhead in Wiltshire, where her half-brother, Richard Colt Hoare, was continually improving his splendid grounds. In the evening she would sing and play the piano, organ, or harp, and many volumes of music survive, inscribed with her name and scribbled with her pencilled notes.

Education was a subject which interested both her husband and herself. A school was built just outside the park fence, where little girls in red cloaks learned their letters from the dame in charge, and no doubt submitted their needlework for Lady Acland's inspection. Broadclyst presented a more difficult problem. Here, as in many other villages, 40 or 50 children crowded into a parish room every day to learn from a master who, though 'labouring all day and all the week long like a Horse in a Mill', was quite unable to teach them anything. Acland had already heard of the improved system of teaching with monitors, lately introduced by Andrew Bell, and decided to try it out. He imported a Bell-trained 'lad from London' and sent the Broadclyst master to study under Dr. Bell himself, all at his own expense. Then, with the help of a public subscription, he built a fine new school in the village, to be run on modern lines. It was a great success.[1] 'It is truly a pleasure to see with what alacrity the Children come to School,' wrote the headmaster. 'Their Parents have much difficulty in keeping them at home . . . the Master has witnessed a Group of them assembled together out of school hours around one of their party as a Teacher, and reading and spelling in play . . . such is the effect this Plan is calculated to produce.' It was a bold initiative for a man of 22, bearing in mind that the school's foundation-stone was laid on 25 October 1809, two years before the establishment of the National Society for the Education of the Poor. 'You are taking the lead,' wrote Dr. Bell. 'I trust your example will be followed far and wide.'

For recreation, Acland relied on sketching and travel, often combining the two with an energy that bordered on restlessness. Many volumes of his monochrome sketches survive as witnesses to a period when journeys were made on horseback or in a carriage or sailing-boat, and there was time to pause with a sketch-book and to work up the drawings in the evening. Lydia was usually his companion, and as soon as the children were old enough they came, too. Little Tom made his first family expedition when he was three, in the summer of 1812, while his year-old brother, Arthur, was left at home. It was the Aclands' second trip to Ireland in two years, the attraction being a double one: not only was the scenery splendid for sketching, but also at Belle Vue, in County Wicklow, the Latouche family kept open house for Alexander

Knox and Bishop Jebb, the two outstanding religious thinkers who had already made such an impression on Acland at Hannah More's house. At that 'seat of rest for mind and body', as a friend called Belle Vue, he found a household where Protestant and Catholic servants knelt down together for family prayers, and where religious and philosophical discussion was conducted on a higher plane than he had ever known. From Knox and Jebb he learned that genuine religious commitment need not involve bigotry or intolerance, and the lesson lasted him for the whole of his life.

From Ireland the Aclands made their way to Scotland. A third baby was expected in the autumn, but Lydia was quite undaunted, even when it was proposed to extend the tour to St. Kilda—the remote island on the edge of the Outer Hebrides —where a handful of inhabitants lived by eating the sea-birds which screamed round the precipitous cliffs. Acland was shocked by the islanders' poverty, and spoke earnestly with them before sketching their wretched huddle of thatched huts ('the main square'), and returning to his boat with a firm promise to come again. Lydia was reputedly the first lady ever to land on St. Kilda, and it must have been a great adventure for her: as for little Tom, it remained his earliest memory. However, the most exciting event of the trip was yet to come: on the return journey through Scotland, which included an ascent of Ben Nevis, Acland was met by a messenger from his mother. There was likely to be an opening for him to stand for parliament at the approaching general election, and he must go to Killerton immediately. It was news which he welcomed gladly.

The Young Member for Devon

The county of Devon was at that time a single large constituency, represented by two M.P.s. The electorate of 5,000 was limited to clergy and freeholders, each of whom had two votes, and was obliged to come to Exeter, the single place of voting, in order to cast them in public at the hustings in Castle Yard. There was no secrecy whatever about the proceedings, and little constraint on the amount spent by candidates on getting their supporters to the poll by offering free transport and hospitality. In this instance, the sitting members were John Pollexfen Bastard of Yealmpton, and Sir Lawrence Palk, the developer of Torquay, both substantial Tory landowners. Sir Lawrence had now decided not to seek re-election, and his supporters chose Acland as a suitable successor. Some ineffective opposition by 'a Mr Graves' was withdrawn and, in spite of a wet polling day on 15 October 1812, Sir Thomas found himself a member of parliament for Devonshire, alongside Mr. Bastard. Life for the Aclands now settled into an ordered pattern based on parliamentary sessions: not very onerous, when the sporting seasons took priority and parliament seldom met between July and February. For six months of the year they were free to spend time at Killerton and Holnicote, or to travel abroad. For the sessions they would move up to London, either taking a house, or staying in lodgings at a family hotel, such as Grillion's in Albemarle Street, where the famous dining club had begun to meet. Acland and his lifelong friend, Robert Inglis, were founder members of this club, which derived from the old Christ Church Debating Society and drew together distinguished men from both political parties: they are commemorated in a set of portrait drawings, which Acland commissioned and which were later engraved. The mixture of convivial dinners and lively discussions afterwards exactly suited his temperament. A member said of the club's genial neutrality that[2] 'if the Reminiscences of Grillion's were interleaved with Hansard's debates, I do not believe that any human being would believe in the fidelity of both reports'.

Hansard's reports certainly made gloomy reading when Acland first entered parliament under Lord Liverpool's premiership. England was long overdue for reform in every department of public life. Having embarked on the Industrial Revolution, the country had outgrown most of its archaic laws and institutions. Men were still hanged for poaching, prisoners slept on bare boards, and lunatics were held for years in chains. Parliament only represented a fraction of the people and elections were mostly won by bribery and patronage. The Civil Service was just as corrupt. Yet it seemed impossible for the government to take any action. Since the 'Glorious Revolution' of 1688, the Whigs had been regarded as the people's party, but now they were deeply distrusted because of their supposed revolutionary sympathies. The horrors of the guillotine were still sufficiently fresh in most men's minds to act as a brake on progress, however moderate, and any suggestions for reform were looked on with suspicion. Acland, who was instinctively progressive and humane, felt uneasy in this situation. Although he was deeply rooted in Tory tradition, he soon showed his supporters that they had sent a young man to Westminster who was not afraid to express his own opinions. As early as March 1813 he was up on his feet in the Commons, speaking earnestly in favour of Catholic Emancipation, and drawing on his own experiences in Ireland to plead for tolerance. It cost him the friendship of neighbours and constituents. In the next session he spoke on easing the Norwegian blockade (again using personal experience), improving the state of London prisons, and relieving the 'German Sufferers' who had been left in Napoleon's wake—always urging the liberal case when others in his party were for keeping charity at home, or leaving things as they were.

With the summer recess of 1814 came a complete break from politics for the Aclands. Napoleon had been captured, the war seemed over, and the Continent was open at last. Lady Acland had recovered from the birth of her fourth child, Lydia Dorothea, and on the spur of the moment Sir Thomas decided to take her and five-year-old Tom to Vienna, where all the great people of Europe were gathering for the Peace Congress. Having been vaccinated, the party set off in a brand-new carriage 'painted a fine new patent yellow picked out in black', with the family coat of arms gleaming on the doors. It was a typical Acland jaunt, made without much regard to expense or duty to constituents, but enjoyed with gusto. In Vienna, introductions from England ensured that the Aclands were soon able to join in the brilliant social life which the Congress had attracted, and they took a house for the winter. 'What do you do about Church?' wrote Henrietta anxiously from Devon. Sir Thomas learned German and made many new friends, among them Archduke John of Austria, and von Hammer, the historian. 'We went the other night to Prince Metternich's, where there was such a tribe of Kings and Queens that one felt in continual danger of tumbling over some of them,' wrote Lydia to her mother. 'The Hackney Coaches are on Sledges.' She learned Italian, took singing lessons and taught Tom the rudiments of Latin. Her portrait, painted by Lawrence just before this expedition, shows how handsome she was at this period (Plate XI); she even admitted to her mother that she 'produced a most brilliant effect' in the jewels and brocades which had been bought on the way through Paris. A sharp change of mood followed when the party returned home in February 1815, and found England sunk in the depths of post-war depression. Acland's constituents were waiting for him with petitions begging parliament to fix the price of corn at a level high enough to benefit the farmers and landlords. He was persuaded that to do so would also benefit the whole community. 'The poor-houses,' he declared in the House, were 'filled with agricultural labourers deprived of their usual employment in consequence of the discouragement of agriculture.' Similar petitions were pouring in from all parts of the country, and before the end of the session the notorious Corn Laws had been passed. There was no more travelling that year. Lydia's fifth child, Henry Wentworth, was born in August, and the family divided their time between Killerton and Holnicote. For the session of 1816 the Aclands took a house in Pall Mall, 'an excellent house, and nicely furnished', noted the rector of Selworthy, who occasionally came up to London. It was convenient for Lydia that her parents were within easy reach at Mitcham, so that she could go to them for the next child's birth (Harriet, who never thrived, and who died when she was a year old), and settle seven-year-old Tom into a preparatory school nearby.

Sir Thomas was beginning to earn a reputation as an active parliamentarian and a fluent speaker, and at the start of the session he was invited by Castlereagh to move the address of thanks to the throne—a sign that he was considered something of a coming man. Though agricultural distress was the question of the day, and he had a handful of petitions from Devon to present on the subject, he was not concerned solely with constituency matters: he also spoke freely on the extravagance of the royal family, the bad conditions in the cotton mills, the 'horrible and infamous slave-trade' which still 'flourished outside British territory, and other subjects which stirred his conscience. His constituents did not always appreciate his independent standpoint or his absences abroad during the recess (a second trip to the Tyrol took place in the summer of 1816), and an exasperated friend summed up the general feeling when he wrote, 'Honestly, if I were a Devonshire gentleman I should think you treated the County a little cavalierly . . . [they expect] to see their Member in the summer—that he should live among them, and spend his money among them and make his appearance at their public meetings—you do nothing of all this.' The rebuke came home at the general election of 1818 when he found his position challenged by Lord Ebrington, heir to the Whig Lord Fortescue. A contested election was then a costly affair, and Acland and Edmund Bastard, his fellow sitting member, decided to pool their funds in coalition. Ebrington, on the other hand, offered free transport and hospitality only to those who would promise to 'plump' (vote) for him and him alone. Thanks to his 'glorious army of Plumpers' who poured in from every part of the country, Ebrington topped the poll. Bastard, who had never uttered a controversial word in parliament, came second, and Acland retired from the contest on the third day. 'It would teach him to incline his ear to the voice of his constituents,' commented a sardonic observer. It was his only defeat in a long parliamentary career, and it was soon avenged, When George III's death in 1820 precipitated another general election, Acland's supporters did not scruple to use personal abuse of Ebrington, alluding to his small stature and halting speech as well as his supposedly dangerous radical opinions. This time there was no coalition with Bastard, and Acland in turn went out for plumping votes. The result was that, in a low poll, he easily came top, with Bastard second, and Ebrington retired from the contest. The carriage, decorated with crimson moreen and oak-leaves, swept back to Killerton in triumph and '*Acland for Ever*' was the motto of the day.

   In some ways the two years' rest from parliament had done the whole family good. Lady Acland was very unwell after her little girl's death, and even by October she was only able to go round the shrubbery at Killerton in a bath-chair: she must have welcomed the chance to recover her strength before the next baby, Peter Leopold, was born in the following year. The other children were growing up. Tom at preparatory school, and Arthur a pupil with the Broadclyst curate, were getting ready to follow their father to Harrow; Baldwin was destined to enter the Navy as a twelve-year-old midshipman under his uncle Charles, and little Lydia, Henry and Leopold were still in the nursery, where three more babies eventually joined them. The family centred on Killerton, migrating for several weeks every Christmas to Holnicote, where the black-game shooting, the carol-singers, and the school feast were all part of the season's pattern. It became an invariable custom, whenever they were at Holnicote, to lunch at the rectory on Sunday, and walk up Selworthy Combe with Mr. Stephenson after the service, and the children recalled in later years the impressive way in which their father would discuss the sermon and declaim his favourite hymns, as he strode vigorously up the hill. Because his own boyhood had been spent at Holnicote, the place was always Acland's favourite, and he made closer contact with his children there than he did anywhere else. Certainly they all remembered it to the end of their lives, with the special affection that belongs to happy holiday places. At Killerton the atmosphere was stiffer. The newly bow-fronted dining-room often held 18 or 20 people sitting down to turtle soup and venison—the company probably including some of the numerous Acland, Hoare and Fortescue relations, as well as old friends, political supporters and county neighbours, of whom Lord and Lady Clifford, the great Catholics of Devon, were particular friends on account of Sir Thomas's support of Emancipation. William Wilberforce came to stay, and departed saying, 'I love Acland!'; Archduke John of Austria was obliged to cancel a visit, but presented a portrait of himself to be hung at Killerton, for the trips to the Tyrol and Vienna had resulted in a warm friendship. The artists Francis Nicholson and Henry Singleton came to the house to paint the family, and the huge full-length portrait of Sir Thomas by William Owen was commissioned by the Tory committee as a consolation prize for his election defeat. Of estate business there was no end, even though detailed management was handled by stewards, bailiffs and lawyers, and a 'Justice Room' was made at Killerton in which Acland could carry out his duties as J.P. When he attended the quarter sessions in Exeter he would sometimes take Lady Acland to the new Institution Room in the Cathedral Close, which he had helped to establish, to hear a concert by the Harmonic Society, for music was her main recreation in a life still much dominated by the nursery. All in all, the two years after Sir Thomas's defeat were valuable, for they brought him into closer contact with his family and estates, and West-Country public affairs than had ever been possible before.

When Sir Thomas re-entered parliament in April 1820 he found that the political climate had changed to one that was much more congenial to him. Matters had recently come to a head: two violent events—the shooting down of the Manchester mob by the military at 'Peterloo', and the revolutionary Cato Street Conspiracy to blow up the members of the Cabinet as they sat at dinner—had shocked the Tories and divided them into reactionary and progressive groups. There was a growing number who now accepted that reform was necessary, and asked themselves, with Acland, 'whether danger was likely to be lessened by keeping back what must eventually conceded'. On both sides of the House, party boundaries were dissolving and re-forming into new patterns (eventually to emerge as the Liberal and Conservative parties of later years), and the moderate Tories, of whom Acland was one, often had more in common with the moderate Whigs than with the reactionaries on their own side of the House. In such an atmosphere Sir Thomas was able to exercise his conscience freely, and in the 10 years which led up to the death of George IV in 1830 he increased his reputation for independence, characteristically disagreeing with his friends when necessary. He pleaded for generosity to Queen Caroline when Wilberforce had utterly condemned her, spoke with disgust of the savage Game Laws (which to his fellow-landlords seemed such a normal part of life), and supported a measure to reduce the high duties on imported corn which were so popular with Devon farmers. However, his main preoccupation was with religious liberty, one of the burning questions of the day. The Established Church still held a monopoly of public positions which had hardly changed since the Anglican Settlement of 1689 had welded Church and State into one. Even to become a J.P., let alone anything more important, it was necessary to receive the Anglican sacrament, whether one believed in it or not. This went very much against the grain with Sir Thomas. He had declared himself an enemy to religious intolerance from the moment he entered the House, and he was now at a point in his career when his opinions carried some weight: remarkably ecumenical opinions they were, for a staunch churchman of the period. Remembering the lessons in tolerance which he had learned from Jebb and Knox, he applied them equally to Catholics and nonconformists, and even within his own church managed to steer clear of party spirit, supporting High-Church Joshua Watson and his 'Hackney Phalanx' in their tireless efforts to build new schools and churches at home, just as heartily as he joined his old Evangelical friends of the Clapham Sect in their struggle to abolish slavery and to set up missions abroad. His simple test of other men's beliefs was their sincerity. This attitude guaranteed him respect. He was dubbed the 'leader of the religious party in the House of Commons' by Sir Walter Scott when Wilberforce retired from parliament in 1825, and some of his best speeches were made in support of the liberalising measures which now followed: the Dissenters' Marriages Bill, the repeal of the Test and Corporation Acts (a Whig measure) and, in 1829, the Catholic Emancipation and Disenfranchisement Bills which finally put an end to the scandal of Catholic disabilities. The debate on the last of these was emotional and divisive, and Acland found himself in opposition to many of his friends—notably Robert Inglis, who, on this issue, had ousted Peel from his Oxford University seat. In Clapham, an Evangelical friend cut down Sir Thomas's picture from the wall, and Hannah More spoke severely of her 'recreant Knight'. The Bills were passed by large majorities, thanks to Tories like Peel and Wellington, who changed sides at the last moment. Acland was no recent convert: he could look back over 16 years to his maiden speech, and justifiably take some of the credit for the fact that, as he said, in a county which had for a long time been decidedly hostile to the Roman Catholics, he had the satisfaction of witnessing the gradual removal of that hostility.

If his 'manly and consistent stand', as Lord Ebrington described it, strained old friendships, it also brought new allies. In the general election of 1830 which followed George IV's death, Acland was strongly supported by the Whigs, and found himself elected a close second to Ebrington, with Bastard at the bottom of the poll. The issue of the day was electoral reform—now so strongly demanded throughout the country that it was impossible to postpone it any longer. The Whigs had always wanted it, and many Tories were prepared to agree: many others were wavering. Only the Duke of Wellington's 'Ultras' refused to give any ground, and when the Duke resigned his premiership, in the face of the new parliament's pressure, the Whig ministry was formed under Lord Grey with the object of bringing in a Reform Bill. Acland's position was not so definite as it had been in the question of religious liberty: he described himself as 'a Reformer on principle', but he was a conservative reformer who did not go all the way with Grey's proposals to disenfranchise the boroughs and extend the electorate. Nevertheless, he thought it right to vote for the critical second reading of the Reform Bill on 22 March 1831. The question was 'Reform or no Reform', he declared: if modifications were needed, they could come in committee. Members who professed themselves friendly to the Bill, but refused to vote for it because of minor objections, would find themselves classed as 'decided opponents and stoppers of Reform'. Speaking almost last in the debate, to a full and tense House of Commons, Sir Thomas may well have influenced the waverers: in any event, the second reading was passed by a majority of one. He could have claimed that decisive vote as his.

The Bill was defeated almost as soon as it got into committee on an amendment which Acland's conscience compelled him to support: the measure was withdrawn, and parliament dissolved. He found himself facing the electors yet again, but they were now in a very different mood. His actions had pleased nobody: the Tories considered that his support for the reading of the Bill was tantamount to treason, while the Whigs were disgusted because he had voted for the amendment. He felt bitterly that there was no room for his own middle road, and decided that the only honourable course was to withdraw from politics altogether. The county of Devon was, he stated in a letter to his constituents, 'very much divided into two parties holding very opposite opinions, the one so ready to adopt any innovation and the other as slow to consent to any improvement'. To maintain an independent footing was becoming an almost hopeless task, and he preferred a 'painful sacrifice to a disgraceful compromise'.

No one doubted that the sacrifice was sincerely made, but it certainly saved Acland from defeat in an election which turned out to be a Whig landslide. Lord Ebrington and the radical Lord John Russell were elected unopposed for Devon, and the landed families—Northcotes of Pynes, Kekewiches of Peamore, Kennaways of Escot, and Fursdons of Fursdon—who had been the Tory mainstay, had to watch helplessly while a second and decisive Reform Bill was made law in 1832, followed by a programme of legislation which included Abolition of Slavery, Poor Law Reform, establishment of the Ecclesiastical Commission, and the first effective Factory Act. All these were of the deepest interest to Acland, and, if he had remained in parliament, he might well have been marked out for promotion by Peel who, as Leader of the Opposition in the Commons, was now re-shaping the Tory party under the new title of 'Conservative'. As it was, he had put himself out of the running. Whether or not he intended his retirement to be permanent is not clear, but in the event he was only away from Westminster for six years. It was a period which he afterwards recalled as the happiest time of his life.

The Happy Interlude

The family was now complete and thriving. Lady Acland had fully recovered her health after her years of child-bearing, and, except for little Harriet's death, no serious illness or bereavement had yet broken the immediate circle. Reginald, John Barton, and Agnes (four, eight and 10 years old respectively) were still in charge of nurses and governesses; Leopold was preparing for Harrow, where Henry was now a senior boy; Baldwin was at sea, and Tom, who had come of age in the previous year, was at Christ Church with Arthur. Lydia Dorothea was old enough to go to dinner-parties in London as 'Miss Acland'. The parents ruled over this large family with an unquestioned authority. It was taken for granted that Tom should not be allowed to train for a profession, because he was heir to the property, and that Arthur should be forbidden to enter the Church as he so much wished. Later, John Barton only succeeded in emigrating to New Zealand in the face of much discouragement. Such parental tyranny was typical of the time, and was accepted the more readily in this case because of the real warmth and concern which lay behind it. There was a good deal of sympathy between father and sons in the matter of politics: nothing could have pleased Sir Thomas more than the understanding letter which Tom wrote on the occasion of his father's decision to retire, unless it was the news that his son had taken a double first-class degree in classics and mathematics. Christ Church was, in any case, about to confer an honorary D.C.L. on Sir Thomas in June, and both parents went up to Oxford for Commemoration. Tom wrote in his diary that his chief pleasure in 'this week of vanity' was seeing his father and mother so happy.

As with his family, so with his estates, Acland ruled with benevolent despotism, and received unquestioning loyalty in return. Broadclyst was full of improvements. The church was undergoing repairs of a disastrously thorough nature. 'What is in that cart?' asked Sir Thomas, as he saw the remains of the wagon-roof and rood-screen being taken through the village. 'If you please, Sir Thomas, angels!' was the reply. At Killerton an orangery had been built, and Veitch's planting was beginning to come to maturity: there were new entrance gates and a lodge, and more additions to the house. The place had become a favourite subject for local artists. Holnicote estate also had been developed: the hills behind Selworthy were now planted with trees (a plantation for each child's birth); there was a network of new paths for the Sunday walks, and a little group of thatched cottages had been built on the Green for estate pensioners, following the example of Acland's friend, John

Harford at Blaise Castle, and owing something to the picturesque style of Belle Vue in Ireland. As at Killerton, there was a
school, where the little girls wore red cloaks and were given a
Christmas dinner. The Cornish properties, Trerice and Bude,
had always been difficult to manage because of distance, but
here, too, Acland had laid out a good deal of money, building a
breakwater and canal at Bude to improve the little harbour,
and converting 'Efford', a fisherman's cottage, into a holiday
retreat for the family. There was also a new church. Added
to the expense of a large family, a series of costly elections,
and massive contributions to charity, all this outlay was greatly
in excess of Acland's resources, and every year the position was
getting worse. There was no difficulty in borrowing money,
thanks to Hoare's bank and the security of the land, but he was
wretchedly aware that he was now spending more on loan
interest than on all his estates put together. It was presumably
with economy in mind that he decided to buy a yacht in 1834:
perhaps he thought that holidays afloat would be cheaper for
the family than foreign travel, but his Hoare relations laughed
at the idea, and it certainly did nothing to improve his finances.

His interest in yachting had started two years earlier, when
the family was at Holnicote for the whole summer in order to
escape an outbreak of cholera in Exeter. Allerford House, half
a mile away, was let to Captain Fairfax Moresby, R.N., who
had commanded a ship engaged in putting down the slave trade,
and was now, like many other naval officers of the time, settled
down with his family for a period on half-pay. Sir Thomas
cherished the memory of his own brother, Captain Charles
Acland, who had died of blackwater fever a few years earlier
in the course of the same duties, and he found much in common with Captain Moresby. An introduction to the pleasures
of sailing soon followed. Mr. Stephenson, who kept a faithful
diary, recorded that on 9 August 1832 the Aclands went to
Porlock Weir 'to take a trip in a sort of yacht they have hired'.
This vessel was named *Arrow*, and so quickly did the family
catch yachting fever that in the next two weeks four voyages
were made in the Bristol Channel, some of them in extremely
rough weather. Everything about the adventure—freedom from
convention,   new   opportunities   for   sketching—appealed

enormously to Sir Thomas, and next summer he hired another
yacht, *Vansittart,* in which, with Captain Moresby, his wife
and four of his sons, he embarked on a three-week trip round
the coast of Ireland, sketching all the way, in high delight. As
if that were not enough for one summer, the party was off
again a bare three days after reaching home, bound for the coast
of northern Spain, with Moresby, Lady Acland, Dorothea, and
the two youngest children on board. Perhaps this was the best
voyage of all: at San Sebastian the party left the yacht and
travelled 100 miles inland to the highest part of the Pyrenees
where, as Acland proudly recorded, he and his wife made the
ascent of Mount Bergan on foot. His sketches of the mountain
(some of the best he ever did) convey very strongly the triumph
of that moment, and the feeling of complete freedom which
they were enjoying. It must have been their happiest time since
the trip to Vienna, 20 years before. The yacht sailed as far as
Vigo Bay before turning for home, pausing on the way to see
the battlefield of Corunna. They were out for seven weeks.
On 21 September Mr. Stephenson heard the yacht's single
gun in Porlock Bay, and by nine o'clock the whole party were
sitting down to dinner at Holnicote. The first small shadow
now fell across the family happiness. 'Miss Acland,' noted the
rector, 'was not quite well.' It was the start of a long progressive
illness (possibly muscular dystrophy), which was to condemn
Lydia Dorothea to a lifetime of invalidism.

During the winter, which was spent mostly at Holnicote
(Exeter again being visited by cholera), Acland resolved to
acquire a boat of his own. With the encouragement of Captain
Moresby and his own midshipman son, Baldwin, he bought, at
Dartmouth, a two-masted schooner of 186 tons, built for the
fruit trade, and converted her into a yacht capable of accommo-
dating the whole family as well as a paid crew. The equipment
on board included enough cutlery and glass to supply a large
household, as well as Lady Acland's piano. On 2 August 1834
The Lady of St. Kilda, as she was named in honour of Lady
Acland's earlier exploit, sailed on her maiden voyage, which
was to be a circumnavigation of England and Scotland. Except
for Tom, who was travelling in Europe, the entire Acland family
was on board, and Captain Moresby was in command.

From the cabin roof swung a tray holding the sketching materials with which Acland made a pictorial log of the journey as the yacht sailed up the east coast and around Cape Wrath, making a special detour to revisit the island of St. Kilda. Acland found a resident minister with a church and a manse, but little improvement otherwise: he left behind a prize of £20 for the islander who first built himself a proper house. The daily sketches show a coastline which the age of steam had hardly touched. Even at Liverpool the old dock was crowded with square-rigged ships, and there was only a scattering of steam packets among the sailing vessels in the river. The marshy banks were still lined with windmills. Sir Thomas believed in teaching his sons discipline by making them do the hard work on the ship, and life on board was tough. 'To tell you how gladly I leave this yacht and all the whole life and habits of the sea would be difficult,' wrote Arthur to his future wife. 'I am glad to come below, as canvas shirt and trousers and bare feet are not warm.' Sir Thomas, however, remained in the highest spirits, and when the six weeks' voyage was over, and the yacht laid up for the winter at Porlock Weir, he was already beginning to make plans for the following year.

He was keen to explore the Peninsula as far as Lisbon, where Baldwin was stationed as a lieutenant in H.M.S. *Stag*, but Dorothea's health had to be considered. Her illness had not responded to any of the remedies prescribed for her, and in the spring of 1835 the doctors suggested wintering abroad. Sir Thomas decided to take the yacht to the Mediterranean in the autumn, and to spend the winter in Rome. First, however, he was resolved that the excursion to Lisbon and the Peninsula should go ahead, and the yacht sailed in May with his wife and Arthur as passengers—the latter a reluctant one, for he was waiting to be married and grudged the three months away from his fiancée, Fanny Williams. He became exasperated by the high spirits of his father, who insisted on sailing into Lisbon without running up any colours, so as to surprise Baldwin in H.M.S. *Stag*. 'The consequence was two blank shots from the Guard-ship, succeeded by two real shots,' wrote Arthur to Fanny, 'the next one would have been on board and perhaps cost us a man.' The weather was so bad on the return voyage that even the sailors were sick, and the party was probably glad to see Porlock Bay again on 3 September. There was only a month at home before the yacht sailed again with Sir Thomas and Lady Acland, both their daughters, and nine-year-old Reginald on board: 'We never slept on shore till the 12th or 14th January in Rome,' recalled Acland, 'and we started again on Rennie's [Reginald's] birthday, the 23rd April, 1836, and with one day's exception only . . . did not sleep on shore again until we reached our home in the Month of August.' The three-month stay in Rome was full of enjoyment. It was a fashionable wintering place for English people, and a great centre for artists and intelligentsia of many nations. Baron Bunsen, the Prussian ambassador for the last 20 years, had made his villa into a salon for Protestant society: Acland and Bunsen were soon on excellent terms and the friendship proved to be a lasting one. Lady Acland had brought her music, and often had the distinction of playing and singing before the Danish sculptor Thorwaldsen, who worked in Rome. She marked the book of songs 'The Traveller' as a reminder, and Sir Thomas brought back copies of Thorwaldsen's famous medallions, 'Night' and 'Morning', to adorn the walls of Killerton. He spent much time in seeing the sights, including the 'curious catacombs for the preservation of the Body after Death', and practised the rules of architectural perspective: there were no crowds to spoil the view of the Coliseum which he sketched from Dorothea's bedroom, where Miss Hill, the governess, looked after her and taught the younger children their lessons. Tom and Henry, who were both travelling on the Continent, joined the yacht for the journey home, and the whole expedition was a great success. 'I do not recollect that I ever had a more thorough *family* enjoyment than when I spent ten months on board *The Lady of St. Kilda,*' wrote Sir Thomas to a great-niece many years later. 'I drank the Queen's health in a mulled, i.e., warm, bottle of old Port on the top of Mount Etna at sunrise of the Glorious First of June 1836'—the only night he spent ashore on the return trip. A sketch records the typically exuberant episode. But the letter was written at the end of his life, and his memory had slipped: it was not until June 1837 that Queen Victoria was on the throne, and by that time a more sombre chapter in the family's history had begun. The happy interlude was over.

Honourable Member for North Devon

The whole family gathered at Killerton when the travellers arrived home at the end of July: Arthur, who now was married and with a baby due, was the only absentee. Thanks to the extraordinarily complex network of solicitors, agents, stewards and servants to whom Sir Thomas was able to delegate most of his responsibilities, nothing much had gone wrong at home after what was virtually 14 months' absence. Unhappily, Dorothea was very little better for the trip, and was now obliged to resign herself to a life spent mainly on the sofa, remaining, nevertheless, the cherished confidante of her brothers, and a wonderful embroideress, whose achievements are still among the family possessions. Tom, at 27, was longing to be in parliament, but had conscientiously turned down several invitations to stand, and obeyed his father's commands to travel and study instead. The same over-conscientiousness, stemming from an intensely religious upbringing, characterised Arthur, who had already embarked on a life of good works which was to have fatal effects on his health, and Henry, who had temporarily broken down under the strain of his first year at Christ Church. All three brothers had been much influenced by the Tractarian religious revival at Oxford, which did not please their mother. With the change of middle life, her evangelical views, always much less flexible than her husband's, had hardened into something like an obsession, and she did not hide her contempt for the fasting, surplices, emblems, use of the crucifix and other outward signs of the movement. The family avoided the subject whenever possible, but the atmosphere at Killerton was uncomfortable. In particular, Lady Acland disapproved of Mary Mordaunt, whom for five years Tom had longed to marry, considering her family too 'fine', wordly and Tractarian. She managed to veto the marriage for a further five years, and even then forbade Tom's brothers to attend the early communion which preceded the service. Sir Thomas was made miserable by the tension, being, as a friend said, 'exactly between the two parties'. He appreciated the religious verse of John Keble, the initiator of the Tractarian movement, and had championed his *Christian Year* when it first appeared, but the more extreme views of Pusey and Newman seemed to tend too strongly in the direction of Rome, and he drew back from them. He felt far more at home discussing religion with plain-thinking Mr. Stephenson or Mr. Bond, the chaplain at Killerton.

It had long been in his mind to build a new chapel nearer to the house than the old building at Columb John, and now that he was home again he lost no time in putting his plan into action. He had decided on a site 12 years earlier, and settled that the architect should be C. R. Cockerell, who had already carried out some work on the estate: he was celebrated for his classical style, but on this occasion was persuaded to copy a Norman chapel at Glastonbury which had caught Sir Thomas's fancy. The contract dragged on for three years, and the final account greatly exceeded the architect's estimate, but on 21 September 1841 Killerton chapel, dedicated to the Holy Evangelists, was consecrated. Its whole style reflected the views of its patron. The seats were arranged along the walls, in rows facing each other, so that he could see the entire congregation of family, servants, estate workers and tenants, all sitting in their appointed places, while Mr. Bond read the very plain service. Sir Thomas himself was the presiding figure. Here, in miniature, was society as he wished it to be: a paternalistic hierarchy, held together by the cohesive element of Christianity and expressed in corporate worship. Here he could believe in Church and State as one. It was an ideal which he carried into all his public work.

At 50 he felt ready for parliament again. The Reform Bill had divided Devon into two, each part returning two members, and at the general election of 1837, brought about by William IV's death, Sir Thomas was invited to stand for North Devon alongside Lord Ebrington. He accepted, was returned without a contest, and represented the constituency for 20 years with no opposition. The same election brought Tom into the House for the first time, as member for West Somerset. However, there was little joy in the occasion, for a double blow now struck the family: news came that Baldwin had died at sea of blackwater fever while engaged in putting down the East African slave trade, and, almost at the same time, little Reginald succumbed to measles at school. These were the first in a series of bereavements which were to shadow the next two decades, all borne with a resignation and fortitude which sprang from an utterly unshaken faith in the hereafter.

Lady Acland went less to London in this second phase of her husband's career, and Tom, until he married, kept his father company in town. He was soon elected to Grillion's Club, which maintained its old cross-bench character and had recently celebrated its jubilee with a dinner at which 28 members got through more than a hundred bottles of wine—Sir Thomas himself contributing some old rum of 1691. He was still a popular secretary of the club, and in 1846 was presented with a splendid silver candlestick nearly three feet high, engraved with the members' names. His many friends forgave him for his unanswered correspondence, undecipherable handwriting and impulsiveness ('a walk in London with Acland is like walking with a grasshopper', wrote Bunsen, who now lived in London), for the sake of his warm, generous heart and proved integrity.

Party boundaries in the Commons were as confused as ever. The political scene had shifted during Acland's six years' absence, and the issue of the day was now the 'Condition of England Question': an England which had been transformed by the Industrial Revolution into a commercial manufacturing nation depending for its wealth on the cheap labour of the new towns in the north and midlands. The Corn Laws kept the price of food high, and the unfettered operation of supply and demand allowed employers to impose any conditions they pleased: small children, as well as men and women, were obliged to accept low wages and long hours of work to keep their families from starvation. The only limits were set by human endurance, and the grim statistics of the time showed how often this was pushed too far. The need for social reform was urgent, and seemed likely to be forced into violent channels by the Chartists and the Anti-Corn Law League. The Whigs, in office since 1832, had reformed much of the machinery of government and Church, but were reluctant to touch factory conditions because of *laissez-faire* theories that interference would be fatal to the country's prosperity. At the same time, old-fashioned Tories on the other side of the House detested changes of principle. Between the two was Peel's new Conservative group which regarded the extremists on both sides as backwoodsmen, and realised that reform was absolutely necessary if England were to avoid a 'convulsion'. Both Aclands were members of this group, which, when Peel took office in 1841, became the party of progress for the next five years.

Sir Thomas's conception of public duty did not include personal ambition. He never tried to catch the Speaker's eye for the sake of delivering a fine oration, but, as an observer remarked, 'was manly and energetic and would make himself heard and felt' on subjects with which he was familiar, such as the new Poor Law (he was on a Board of Guardians at home), agriculture and slave trade (which still flourished outside British territory). His efforts for abolition and his missionary interests had led him to join the African Civilisation Society, whose aim was to teach Africans how to farm, so that they might do without the profitable business of selling slaves. In 1839 an expedition started up the Niger with this aim—a scheme which had something in common with the 'ground-nuts scheme' of 100 years later, and was equally ill-fated. Sir Thomas spoke in the Commons, defending the expedition, to which Samuel Crowther (afterwards the first black bishop) was chaplain. Crowther preached in Killerton chapel on one occasion.

At home, the new towns, without churches or schools, needed missionaries no less than Africa. The Industrial Revolution had come no nearer to him than Tiverton, where he sometimes took visitors to see Mr. Heathcoat's new lace factory, but he listened with horror to Lord Ashley's account in the Commons of mills and mines where children of nine were forced to work 16 hours a day, accidents caused by their falling into machinery while they were asleep being commonplace. He voted steadily for Ashley's Factory Acts, which gradually improved conditions; a long process, when simply to bring in a 10-hour working-day meant weeks of contentious debate, and even a humane man like Peel could argue that such a mild measure would spell disaster to the country's trade.

Sir Thomas had an opportunity to put humane principles into practice in 1844, when the new railway line between Bristol and Exeter came to a halt near Killerton because of some dispute. Many 'navigators' were thrown out of work, and came to him for relief, and he decided to give them employment by cutting a new road up into Ashclyst forest. 'His benevolence was singularly rewarded,' wrote Arthur, 'for the workmen struck upon an ancient and forgotten well with a copious spring.' The field had (and still has) the appropriate name of Halliwell, and water from this holy well was piped to Killerton where it provided a much-needed supply till, two centuries later, the house was connected to the mains. It was typical of Acland's attitude to money that this was undertaken at the very time when he was so worried about his failure to make ends meet that he had written despairingly to his sage friend, Sir Robert Inglis, for advice. Inglis diagnosed philanthropy as a prime cause of the trouble. 'You have gone on day by day, and year by year in benevolent careless self-indulgence,' he wrote, 'giving largely to every case of charity, opening your heart and your purse to every act of kindness,—but not sufficiently considering that the day of self-denial must come: when, in more justice to yourself and your family, present and future, you must restrain yourself. *It is not too late.*' He recommended a programme of retrenchment, but it was quite out of Sir Thomas's power to follow any such course, and he continued much as before. Luckily, the general prosperity which settled on the country by the end of the 'hungry forties' did something to ease his problems, but he was never quite free from anxiety about money.

The ever-growing public opinion that the Corn Laws were at the bottom of England's troubles (only the agricultural interest disagreed) was brought to a head by the Irish famine of 1846, and led to their complete repeal in the summer of that year. For the two Aclands it involved a crisis of conscience which they resolved in different ways. Sir Thomas's position was difficult. He felt responsibility for his agricultural constituents and honestly thought that the Corn Laws were working well: on the other hand, he believed, as he said in the House, 'that when a large portion of the people had

continued for a length of time to demand any particular measure
. . . that measure sooner or later was pretty sure to be carried',
and he saw no point in what he called 'factious opposition'.
He ended one of the longest speeches that he ever made by
saying that he intended to 'hold his own course', but would
support the measure once it was passed, and encourage his
constituents to farm all the better for it. In the end, he
abstained from voting, and the Bill, which irrevocably split
the Tory party, was passed with a comfortable majority. Contrary to expectations, repeal did not result in immediate disaster
for agriculture, but, instead, contributed to the general prosperity which now began to settle on the country, thanks to the
expansion of industry and 35 years of peace. It came to full
flowering with the Great Exhibition of 1851, that palace of
industry which epitomised the mid-Victorian age and seemed
to herald a new millenium.

> Hurrah! for honest Industry, hurrah for handy Skill!
> Hurrah for all the wondrous works achieved by Wit and Will!

sang the poet, Martin Tupper, in the mood of the moment. A
marked catalogue remains to show that Tom and his father
joined the many thousands of people who flocked to the
glass palace, noting down what pleased them—not the least
remarkable item being 'Savage's Alarum Bedstead, a curious
contrivance' which tipped the sleeper suddenly into an upright
position. But the optimism of that spring was soon wiped out
by a chapter of personal disasters which turned 1851 into a
black year for the Aclands.

Sir Thomas's already large family had greatly increased
during the 13 years since his re-entry into parliament. Dorothea
still led what she called a life of 'half-health' at home, and
John Barton was reading law in London. All the others were
married, with 21 children between them. Agnes was the wife of
Arthur Mills, a future member of parliament; Leopold was
ordained, and was now the vicar of Broadclyst; Henry was the
leading medical man in Oxford, and Arthur was preparing to
enter into a family inheritance at Huntsham, near Tiverton.
Tom and his wife, with six children, lived at Tetton, near
Taunton, one of the houses which had been part of the Dyke

endowment. Its drains and water-supply were no better than average, and probably accounted for the epidemic of scarlet fever which struck down the whole family in May. First the three-year-old and then the mother herself died: theirs were almost the first graves in the newly-consecrated little burial ground at Columb John. The doctor-brother and the parson-brother gave what help and comfort they could, and poor Tom took what remained of his family to Holnicote. But trouble followed him, for in August (for the second time in its history), the thatched house burned to the ground. As the final blow in this terrible summer, Leopold's wife died of tuberculosis in September. Sir Thomas gave immediate practical help, by purchasing a modest Georgian house within sight of Killerton, called Sprydon, and adapting it for Tom, so that he could bring up his family within reach of home, and Lady Acland could watch over his five motherless children, while still keeping an eye on the four at Broadclyst vicarage. Visitors to Killerton at this time often found the house full of small orphans.

For a time, home duties weighed more heavily than public ones on Sir Thomas, and he absented himself from Westminster, but (as was said of a later generation), 'religion prevented unhealthy solicitude', and he was soon back in his place at Westminster as vigorous as before. His long parliamentary experience gave weight to the short sensible speeches which he made whenever he considered it worth while, voting steadily meantime for the liberalising measures demanded by public opinion which were now brought in by a succession of Whig, Tory and Coalition governments, and supported by the Peelites. Gradually, the 'Condition of England' was improved, though it was some years before farm workers saw much benefit: in March 1853, Mr. Stephenson 'heard of a John Creech of Luckam [Luccombe, the neighbouring parish] being found dead in the snow on the hill, on his return from Huntsham where he had applied for work'—a 25-mile journey each way.

The rector, who had recently completed his 50th year at Selworthy, was now so infirm that his duties were taken by a curate. Nevertheless, it was at his parsonage that the family usually stayed after Holnicote was burned down. The old

Christmas pattern had gone, but Sir Thomas still came up whenever he could, and often brought Lady Acland with him: together they would visit the school, the pensioners' cottages on Selworthy Green, and the annual distribution of the 'Penny' clothing club. 'The poor were very poor, and Lady Acland very benevolent,' wrote one of the curate's pupils many years later. Sir Thomas kept to his old habit of walking up the hill after church on Sunday, with his dogs and any companions who would go with him, declaiming as he went 'on any conceivable subject, moral, religious, scientific or political which at the moment came uppermost in his mind', went on the same writer, 'always interesting, always fresh, always inclined to talk about three things at once'. Those happy Sundays are commemorated by a stone shelter at the head of Selworthy Combe, inscribed with verses from Acland's favourite religious poets, Heber and Keble. Religious tension no longer plagued the family as it had once done. Lady Acland still held to her own strict principles, and thought it wrong to dance, play cards, or read any books except the Bible, but she was much less critical of her sons' 'high' churchmanship, now that they had left home. She played the organ more in her later years, encouraged by some lessons from Samuel Sebastian Wesley when he was the organist at Exeter cathedral: he dedicated some pieces to her, which he wrote specially for the Killerton organ. Music seems to have been the chief relaxation of her somewhat stiff personality, for all accounts suggest that she commanded great, and even excessive, awe from those around her. However, she made an ideal partner for Sir Thomas, and he depended on her utterly. Perhaps her very rigidity balanced his ebullient impulsive nature. At all events, he was broken with grief when, after 48 years of marriage and bearing him 10 children, the physique which had taken her to the top of mountains and over rough seas with her husband failed at last, and she died suddenly on 23 June 1856, while visiting Agnes in London.

The Killerton Oak

Troubles had never come singly to Sir Thomas (Plate XII), but this time the accumulation was overwhelming. The spring of 1856 had started with the loss of his oldest friend, Sir Robert Inglis, and then came the crushing blow of Lydia's death, followed six weeks later by that of Arthur's wife, Fanny. Finally, Arthur himself died of diphtheria within less than a year. For a time, Sir Thomas felt that his own life had come to an end: 'My path is to the grave, I know', he scribbled over Tennyson's words in his copy of *In Memoriam*. It was literally to Lydia's grave at Columb John that he walked day after day to gaze and meditate, and he kept beside his bed her life-sized portrait, taken after her death by George Richmond. By Christmas 1857, he had so worn himself out with grief that Henry feared for his life, and Tom wrote to his father's old friend, Lord Harrowby, begging him to use his influence and give 'serious advice'. Thanks to the support of his family and friends, Sir Thomas did gradually recover some of his old vigour, but he felt that the mainspring of his life had gone, and when the two-year chapter of bereavement ended in March 1858 with the death of his daughter Dorothea, he made the decision to withdraw from parliament and public life. His period of public service extended back to the Napoleonic Wars, and within three years a statue was put up in Exeter, testifying to the great regard in which he was held by the whole county of Devon. At the same time, John Hele, the Alphington postmaster, wrote a popular song called 'The Killerton Oak', which put the matter in a nutshell, ending with the words

> His council was wise and firm as an oak
> He did what was right and 'twas true what he spoke.

It was the general opinion.

It would be wrong to agree with the obituarist in the local paper that Sir Thomas's years 'glided quietly by', for it was not in his nature to do anything quietly. He was still very vigorous in his seventies, and there were many affairs in which he continued to take an active interest: Grillion's Club, for example (which celebrated its golden jubilee in 1863 with a splendid dinner at which Sir Thomas and Sir James Buller East were the only original members), and the changing scene in parliament, where Tom was now back as a Gladstonian Liberal: 'a tremendous blister' to his father, reported Henry.

His interest in foreign countries was keener than ever, now that John Barton had emigrated to New Zealand; and was engaged in establishing his own branch of the family in a colony which from the start his father had been keen to settle and Christianise. As for the estates, there was never a time when Sir Thomas had enjoyed them more. He went less often to Holnicote after Mr. Stephenson died in 1863, but he loved to stay at Bude, where he had built a house for Agnes and Arthur Mills, and made a special point of going to see 'the great October tide' come in. Perhaps as he watched he recaptured something of his happy days in the yacht. At Killerton, there was a perpetual renewal of his pleasure in the garden. John Veitch, its creator, was dead, but his two sons carried on the thriving nursery business which he had established, and they had begun to send plant-hunters out to the west coast of America and eastern Asia. Killerton, as an ideal trial-ground, was continually enriched by their discoveries. It gave an entirely new interest to Sir Thomas, as he walked round the garden after Sunday morning service in Killerton chapel, to watch the progress of little redwood trees grown from the first packet of seed ever to come from California, and to enjoy the flowering of shrubs which had never before been seen in England. It did not matter if he arrived back late at the house, for everybody was so used to his unpunctuality that Tom, a mile away at Sprydon, would wait to hear the Killerton gong before he left home, if he were going to have luncheon with his father. It was an accepted thing that the old man's life regulated that of everyone around him. Broadclyst had never been so dominated by the family as it was now, with Tom as the squire at Sprydon, Leopold settled in the vicarage, and in the centre of it all 'the aged potentate, surrounded by due retinue of more or less aged domestics', as a newcomer to the family circle put it.[3] Arthur's eight children were divided among the households (16 orphans in all), and Henry, who was now Regius Professor of Medicine at Oxford, sometimes came over to stay, and brought his family. It must have seemed as if the parish was populated with Aclands, when they all went to church at Broadclyst on Sunday afternoons. Sir Thomas might well regard them with pride.

When gout and nose-bleeding began to trouble him, he relied more and more heavily on Mary, Tom's second wife, and Agnes Mills to supervise the running of Killerton. Nevertheless, he remained wonderfully active—'not a white hair on his head, and eyes as bright and full of life as that of any of his grandsons!' commented one observer who saw him at close quarters. He was in his 88th year when he died, quietly and suddenly in his chair, in July 1871, one morning, having been for his usual carriage airing on the day before. His death left a gap in the Devon landscape as if a great tree had fallen.

Chapter Seven

TOM THUMB (1809–1837)

IT WAS TO BE EXPECTED that Sir Thomas's eldest child should be remarkable, and Tom—'Tom Thumb' as Lydia called him—fulfilled the expectation. He more than matched his father in looks and ability, as his portrait and double-first degree testify, and the fact that the degree included mathematics suggests that he inherited some of his mother's banking blood. He repeated the pattern of independence and public spirit which had characterised Sir Thomas. If anything, his conscience was even stronger. Yet, at the end of his life, there was a general feeling among his friends that he had only partly fulfilled his promise. There were some important differences in upbringing to account for this. Sir Thomas had endured a long and strictly controlled minority, but was then free to do what he liked with a large fortune as soon as he was twenty-one. He was probably never obliged to ask permission from anyone during the whole of his adult life. Tom, on the other hand, was financially dependent until he was 62, and, for the whole of that time, had to contend with an overpoweringly dominant father in an age when parents were sacred figures. It was as if he grew up in the shadow of the Killerton Oak, unable to move away, knowing that one day he must supplant it. If he received too little credit for his work, his own diffidence was as much to blame as the uncomfortable Acland conscience, which compelled him to vote for the Repeal of the Corn Laws in 1846 and ruin his political career. In actual fact, his achievements in education were more distinguished than his father's, and when his turn came to be Sir Thomas, he was by far the better landlord.

Tom's first memories were all of travel—first the voyage to St. Kilda at three years old, and then the winter in Vienna two years later, when he put on a jacket and trousers for the first time, learned Latin grammar from his mother and, as Henrietta warned in letters from England, 'was on the highway to being spoilt'. The memories were especially vivid because those were the only occasions, during the whole of his childhood, when he was close to his parents for any length of time. Once home from Vienna, he was back with the governesses and tutors to whom they delegated so many of their parental duties. There was not much chance of spoiling, with his father in the thick of parliament and his mother's attention divided between her ever-growing number of children. He already had four brothers and sisters when he was sent away to preparatory school at seven years old, and by the time he left Harrow at 17 he was the eldest of nine.

He used to speak of his schooldays with a marked lack of warmth. The main effect on him, he told his children, was of being crushed. There was perpetual pressure from school and home to work hard and behave virtuously, with an ever-present threat of punishment for failure, both in this world and the next. The fear of Hell, which was such a powerful weapon of the Evangelists, was never far away. Mr. Roberts of Mitcham flogged boys for coming down last in the morning, for being behindhand with work, or even for sharpening pencils the wrong way round, while Dr. Butler, the headmaster of Harrow, complained to Sir Thomas of the slightest departure from rectitude. Just as Henrietta had done, Lydia bombarded her son with letters of admonition, and if Tom did not reply by return a scolding followed. Something in the style recalls the fact that the women were cousins: 'If you really had serious thoughts respecting *another world* should you not behave with more propriety and circumspection in the *present one?*' she wrote on the occasion of Tom's one and only scrape at Harrow. His father was just as anxious that his son should be a paragon, and letters from both parents never stopped coming. Luckily, Tom's considerable ability enabled him to triumph over the incessant pressure, and he finished up in 1826 as head of the school and the first winner of the Peel Essay Medal. 'Tom has all Harrow under his Thumb!' Sir Thomas told his family in high delight. The price, however, was a heavy one, for Tom was left with an overburdened conscience for life and a crippling deference to his parents' wishes which was excessive even in the context of the time.

Before his son went up to Oxford, Sir Thomas sent him to Cornwall for a year, to study with Thomas Fisher, the vicar of Roche. Mr. Fisher was quite out of the usual run of country clergymen who augmented their income by taking pupils. He was much more interested in abstract speculation than in the classical texts which he was supposed to teach, and his large library included works by the unorthodox Coleridge alongside the biblical commentaries. Coleridge is remembered today mainly for his poetry, but in the late 1820s his metaphysical writings, such as *Aids to Reflection,* were—as Tom recalled in later years—'as the breath of life to young men'. The attraction lay in the fact that, having passed through a number of stages which included Unitarianism, German philosophy, and Pantheism, Coleridge had come to rest at last in a highly personal Christianity, which he expressed in this book of 'Spiritual Philosophy written for young men who wanted to form their religious creed in the light of their own convictions'. It might have been written for Tom. He read Coleridge greedily, held stimulating discussions with Fisher, and went up to Christ Church with his head full of metaphysics.

At Oxford he came under a different spell, for his four years as an undergraduate, followed by nine as a Fellow of All Souls, covered the period when the Tractarian Movement first took shape. It was nothing like a movement when he first went up in 1827, although a new religious spirit was very much in evidence. It was badly needed. The Established Church had come to be little more than an organisation for the spread of religion and morals—whether by preaching personal salvation, as the Evangelicals did, or by building new churches and schools, like the official Commissioners. To the Tractarians, the Church was something different and far greater. Keble, Newman and Pusey, all Oriel men when Tom went up, had the vision of a Catholic (that is, universal) Church as the mystical Body of Christ on earth. They stressed the unbroken chain of ordained priests and bishops which stretched back to His original Apostles. Although she was united to the State, she could only be responsible to God, and any attempt to interfere with her structure, however reasonable—for example, by abolishing 10 useless Irish bishoprics—amounted to an abandonment of Christian faith: Keble's famous Assize Sermon on 'National Apostasy' in 1833 was on this very point. Such a conception carried with it a very 'high' emphasis on the Church and her sacraments, and a revival of spiritual life which had long been lacking. Eventually, some men like Newman felt compelled to follow their conscience into the Roman Church, but the majority of Tractarians carried their teaching into the main bloodstream of the Church of England and thereby much enriched it.

Tom already possessed a copy of Keble's *Christian Year*, a little book of Sunday poems based on the Prayer Book, which was immensely popular. People would read the 'Keble for the day' much as they would read the collect, and it spread church teaching to a circle far outside Oxford. Within the university, Newman's famous Sunday afternoon sermons at St. Mary's were the main influence. They had a direct spiritual quality which owed nothing to dramatic effect or polemics; there was 'nothing like them for going home', said Tom, who, like many other undergraduates, was irresistibly drawn to Newman's views. A visit to Ireland in his first long vacation, to see his father's old friend, Alexander Knox, who, a generation earlier, had been prophesying just such an Anglican revival, confirmed him in his feeling that he was on the right road. He and his brother Arthur, who had joined him at Christ Church, became steadily 'less low church on sound conviction', and by the time they took their degrees both were definitely identified with the Tractarian Movement and its leaders—John Keble, Hurrell Froude, Edward Pusey, and John Henry Newman. Charles Marriott, the son of the curate of Broadclyst and a contemporary of Tom's, was to become one of Newman's close disciples.

During these years, Sir Thomas was busy in parliament with the progressive measures, including Catholic Emancipation, which preceded the first Reform Bill. Politics made a bond between father and son, and it must have been a proud moment for both of them when Tom was elected President of the

Oxford Debating Society (the Union) in 1829. He held this office immediately before his life-long friend and contemporary, William Gladstone, and in the same year both Acland brothers became founder members of Gladstone's 'W.E.G.' Essay Society.

Tom's career at Oxford culminated in 1831 with a double-first degree in classics and mathematics. He was now 22, at the height of his mental and physical powers, and much attached to a beautiful and serious-minded sister of his college friend, Sir John Mordaunt. By rights, he ought to have married, started a family and gone into parliament at once as his father had done, but parental wishes dictated otherwise. Sir Thomas was just embarking on his six-year interlude of supposed economy and his plans did not include marriage or an election for his eldest son; neither did he wish him to train for a profession. It was a most baffling time for poor Tom, who was ordered about in an extraordinary manner, being told by turns to study, travel abroad, and return home—seldom being allowed to settle for long in one place without receiving instructions to move on. He obeyed implicitly ('I am sure that my father is quite right'), in a spirit which owed something to Newman's teaching on self-denial as well as to his own lack of confidence, but he blamed this period for the difficulty in settling down to steady work which he often experienced in later life. After taking his degree he was elected an Examination Fellow of All Souls, an honour which carried no teaching obligations, but gave him splendid rooms and the chance of meeting some of the best minds in Oxford. He found himself on easy terms with Newman and the other leaders of the Tractarian Movement, whose strength was growing. A new recruit was F. D. Maurice, the future Christian Socialist, who proved to be one of Tom's most influential friends.

Tom settled down for a year's reading at All Souls, making frequent visits to the Mordaunt family, who lived within easy reach of Oxford, and becoming increasingly devoted to Mary. In the autumn of 1832 he plucked up courage to ask them all down to Holnicote for a visit of mutual inspection. Their religious views were in perfect accordance with Tom's own (Keble was an old family friend), but much too 'high' for Lady Acland. However, the visit seemed to go well, and Tom and Mary sketched, climbed the hills, and read *The Christian Year* together, but when Tom wrote home in the following spring to ask permission for a formal engagement, the parents responded by ordering him to travel abroad for a year. He was still Tom Thumb to them. He went obediently enough, but, as he travelled through Europe, his thoughts were frequently turning towards Mary, and whether he was on the Drachenfelds or the Capitol Hill he would read his Keble for the day, dwelling on the passages marked 'M.M.', in the assurance that she would be doing the same. Orders from home sent him to Rome for the winter, where he was welcomed by the Prussian diplomat, Baron Bunsen, and the cosmopolitan crowd who gathered in his palace; Philip Pusey, the Tractarian's elder brother, was a link with home. Letters from Newman brought news from Oxford, where events were moving fast with the first publication of the first Tracts on church teaching which gave the movement its name. Now that Tom was abroad, he found that he was looking at religious questions from a wider point of view. Why was it necessary always to be entering into speculation about the Church of England? Why could he not 'feel charity to our Romish brethren without explaining away all their errors'? He talked it over with Bunsen, an enthusiastic Lutheran with large ideas about Protestant unity which were quite at variance with those of the Tractarians. Coleridge's teaching that 'the greatest Spiritual Truths are only to be taken in by the human mind by looking at them from both sides' flashed into Tom's mind as if it were a new thought.

All this happened while Tom was longing for something practical to do, and when Bunsen proposed to take him and Philip Pusey on a tour of German schools he jumped at the idea. Prussia had an educational system which was far ahead of any other: the Bell system was regarded as long out of date, and training colleges for teachers had already been developed. Tom worked at his German from morning till night, planning to spend several months of study at Bonn, and Gladstone, who was already in parliament, wrote to him asking for as much information as could be got. It was all in vain. There was only time for the merest glance at Prussian schools before Sir Thomas sent orders calling him back to

England. There was no sudden emergency. His father simply feared that a course of serious work would make him 'too professional' for a future great landowner, in the same way as he had recently over-ruled Arthur's intense longing to be ordained, because his second son would one day inherit the Acland-linked property of Huntsham, near Tiverton. Neither of the young men questioned their father's decision.

Once back in England, Tom had assumed that he might now be allowed to study law, but it was still forbidden, and more than one invitation to stand for parliament was turned down on grounds of expense. The only possibility was a further spell of study at Oxford. He obeyed, as usual, paid an inconclusive visit to the patient Mary, listened to an impressive sermon by Newman on self-denial, and settled down in All Souls. The Tractarian Movement had now gathered additional strength from Dr. Pusey's Tracts, which were longer and more controversial than any which had gone before. They provoked opposition and there began to be an air of battle campaigning in Oxford. Tom was inevitably drawn into it on the Tractarian side, though his opinions were broadening, and he could discuss with Maurice the dangers of 'the Keble school ossifying the idea of the Church'. Arthur, in law chambers in London, and Henry, now at Christ Church, shared Tom's high-church views, and the three brothers discussed with each other and their sister, Dorothea, the fearful difficulties of fasting at Killerton or of possessing a crucifix. This was the time when Lady Acland was much pained by her sons' opinions, and poor Sir Thomas spoke of 'having his family torn from him' and refused to talk about religion on any terms at all.

Arthur's marriage to Fanny Williams, and the consecration of the new church at Bude in September 1835, brought an interlude of harmony, and shortly afterwards the family sailed for the Mediterranean in the family yacht. It was settled that Tom should join them in Rome for Christmas and stay with them for the return voyage. Henry, who had worked himself into a near-breakdown at Oxford, also went out. While their more extroverted father enjoyed the pleasure of yachting and sightseeing, his sons gloomily reviewed their aims in life. 'I am 26¾ years old,' wrote Tom in his journal, 'living for myself and doing no good to anyone.' Rome had once more helped to put his ideas into perspective, and he saw the danger of becoming exclusive and narrow. He could make little of Dr. Pusey's latest severe Tract on Post-Baptismal Sin, and Maurice, who had now left the Movement, agreed: he wrote to Tom, saying that he now found it impossible to meditate on the 'Our Father' without connecting it with the idea of the Brotherhood of Man. This thought (which afterwards led to the foundation of the Christian Socialists) struck an answering chord in Tom, and marked a turning-point for him. He determined that, when he got back to England, he would leave Oxford and its theological wrangling and go into law chambers in London in preparation for an active parliamentary career. Surprisingly enough, Sir Thomas agreed, paradoxically declaring that this was what he ought to have done in the first place, and when, in the follow-ing summer of 1837, the chance came for both father and son to stand for election, handsome financial backing was forthcoming. Tom felt ready to accept, and after a stiff fight he found himself one of the two members for Holnicote's home constituency, West Somerset. At the age of 28 he was Tom Thumb no longer.

Chapter Eight

THOMAS THE ELEVENTH (1837–1898)

The Member for West Somerset

TOM WAS SURPRISED to find how soon his natural diffidence melted away on the hustings, and how readily he was able to jump up and make his maiden speech in the House of Commons on the spur of the moment. 'He had an abundance of easy and good language to express what he felt,' said his father's friends. He chose the commonplace subject of the Civil List to begin with, but before long he was identified as a champion of the Church and an enthusiast for popular education. The need for a national education system had become one of the most pressing aspects of the 'Condition of England Question' which so greatly preoccupied parliament. In spite of great efforts made by the National Society and its nonconformist counterpart, the British and Foreign Bible Society, only one child in 11 went to school, and in the new manufacturing towns a generation was growing up without learning anything whatever except how to mind the mill machinery and stay awake through a 14-hour shift. The rumblings of the Chartist Movement were alerting everybody to the fact that there now existed an enormous, ignorant and discontented mob which was a potential threat to law and order, and education was seen as a sovereign remedy. Since the Reform Bill an annual government grant had been made to the voluntary societies, but there was now talk of an official body, with direct disposal of public money, to supersede this scheme. Religion must obviously be the main subject on the curriculum, because it was the most effective for inculcating good behaviour, but it mattered very little to the Whig government what sort of religion it was: anything based on the Bible would do. To Tom and the other high-churchmen of the Tory party the issue was quite different. They saw the Apostolic Church as part of the constitution of England, uniquely welded to it by the Act of Settlement of 1701, with a clear duty to educate all her citizens in 'the only true religion'. There was a grudging tolerance for nonconformists, but it was combined with a feeling that they would do much better by coming to Anglican schools. To these passionate churchmen the idea of a secular government scheme constituted a threat, and they conceived a plan to pre-empt it with a system of national (i.e., nationwide) education entirely run by the Church. Tom's short visit to Germany had shown him what efficient modern organisation could do, and together with Gilbert Mathison, a like-minded friend who worked at the Royal Mint, he drew up a tentative scheme.

The whole plan was worked out on a diocesan basis. Training colleges for teachers, on the German pattern, were to be linked to each cathedral, and it was suggested that the students might well become deacons. Choir schools and 'middle' (middle-class) schools would supply future student-teachers, and model church elementary schools would be close at hand for teaching practice. At a lower level, the parish would supply the organisation, and each incumbent would co-operate with his schoolmaster (perhaps also a deacon and an expert in church music) to spread the Faith. All would be responsible to a Diocesan Board of Education, headed by the bishop, who would approve its own inspectors. This was the vision of Acland and Mathison: a complete, sanctified, educational system for an Anglican England where all men shared the same beliefs, and Church and State were one. It was a noble vision, even though it was founded on the conception of a medieval England which no longer existed. They worked it out with a group of M.P.s, including Gladstone and Ashley, and presented it to the Archbishop of Canterbury before combining with the National Society to approach the bishops individually. Though response varied, the scheme was a success from the start, and by June 1839 Tom was able to report, in parliament, that 16 diocesan boards were in action, with 80 more in subsidiary districts. In the following winter, two training colleges were opened: St. Mark's in Chelsea, and, to Tom's special pride, St. Luke's in Exeter, soon to be followed by many more. Tom worked from morning till night, and travelled all over England, as school after school and college after college was built, acting as he said 'like a consulting physician to the Diocesan Boards'. There is no doubt that this quick initiative, for which Tom and Gilbert Mathison were entirely responsible, forestalled any secular government scheme. For better or worse, it was due to them that England's elementary education was mainly run by the churches and chapels for the next 30 years.

Tom felt a great sense of achievement. His feeling of unworthiness began to diminish, and by the end of 1840 he was confident enough to propose to Mary Mordaunt—they were married in the following April. They were the same age and a perfect match; the only pity was that they had held apart from each other for so long. The inscription in the beautiful black velvet-covered Bible, which Dorothea embroidered with pearls and gold thread for a wedding present, conveys some of the affection which the young Aclands felt for one another—all the stronger, perhaps, because of their overbearing parents— and they held out their arms to Mary as their new sister. She responded with equal warmth, and soon became a much-loved member of the family, overcoming with great simplicity and sweetness all Sir Thomas and Lady Acland's prejudice. She did not forget Keble's verse in *The Christian Year:*

> We need not bid for cloistered cell,
> Our neighbour and our work farewell,
> Nor strive to wind ourselves too high
> For sinful man beneath the sky

and her sincerity acted as a calming influence on Tom, who was becoming alarmed at the Rome-ward tendencies of some of his friends, now that Newman had apparently explained away the Thirty-Nine Articles in his recently published *Tract Ninety.*

The couple set up house in London, and very soon the 'chicks', as their father called them, began to appear: seven of them in 10 years. Living on a far less grand scale than the previous generation, it was possible for the parents to keep their children close, and Mary chose to teach them all herself, out of tiny lesson-books which still survive. In the parliamentary recess they moved down to Killerton, Holnicote or Bude, wherever Sir Thomas might be, and shared in the rackety life of a family, where, as the old housekeeper put it there 'was never no time', and all the most important business was transacted after midnight. As for Tom, the happiness of marriage released all the warmth and generosity of his nature. Some of his morbid self-doubt disappeared: there were far fewer notes about religious scruples in his journal, and even his attitude to his parents relaxed when he became a father himself. 'I know not why, I just remembered the Killerton chanting of the evening Psalms with gratitude, and I though how much we owed you', he wrote to his mother in a burst of spontaneous warmth, the morning after his eldest son was born.

The next few years were probably the happiest in Tom's whole life. All the signs pointed to a bright future. Everything around him seemed to expand; his hard work for the National Society was well rewarded, and he began to discover a capacity for enjoyment which was almost equal to his father's. The two had formed a comradely relationship in the House, and, when their opinions differed, Tom was not afraid to vote in the opposite lobby. Education and religion were the two subjects which mainly stirred him to speak. At first, his standpoint was that of a strict Tractarian, but he gradually drew further away from religious controversy, and when Newman was received into the Roman Church in 1845 he was saddened but not bowled over, as he would once have been. A small private 'Brotherhood of St. Barnabas', which he and Arthur had with Gladstone helped to found for the purpose of devotion and good works, began to seem less important than the 'Brotherhood of Man' so much emphasised by Maurice. Tom reflected that it might be as important for the Church to reconcile herself with the modern world as to prove her continuity with the past. In particular, Ashley's speeches on the Factory Bills opened his eyes to an England which the Church had hardly touched. The old parish boundaries were often meaningless; Manchester, for example, with a population of 400,000, was still a single parish in the diocese of York. More than half the people arrested there by the police could neither read nor write. It was plain that the church schools were wholly inadequate, yet Ashley's proposals for government non-sectarian schools met with fierce opposition from reactionary Tory churchmen and let-alone Whigs alike. Tom said in the House that he found both points of view 'intolerably abstract and inhumane'. All his innate liberalism came to the surface, and in a passionate speech of support for Ashley (himself a strong Evangelical) in 1843, he declared that 'he dared not as a member of parliament—he dared not as an Englishman— refuse to take his share of responsibility . . . the State must do what the Church had not done'. It was a turning-point in his development.

From the outset of Tom's parliamentary career, the question of the Corn Laws had presented him with a dilemma. With Francis Dickinson as his fellow-member, he represented a rural constituency in the Tory interest. Most of his supporters were landowners and farmers, and they depended on Protection to keep up the price of corn. Yet Tom was well aware that many poor people in his constituency found it impossible to afford adequate food. 'It is a choice of evils,' said a West-Country journal, 'in which cheap bread is ruin to the agriculturist and dear bread is a calamity to the rest of the population.' Tom felt deeply responsible to both sections. He took great pleasure in his double role of member and future landlord, and he was never happier than when he was talking to the farmers at Holnicote, but he could not help seeing that many of them were farming very badly, and that their labourers were miserably poor. He often discussed the problem with Philip Pusey, the member for Berkshire, who had been a close friend since the winter in Rome. Philip was no 'Puseyite' theologian like his brother, but a keen agriculturist and a landowner who ran his own estate on modern lines. He had inaugurated the Royal Agricultural Society in 1840 and his home farm upon his estate was the scene of many experiments. Originally a Protectionist, he had become more and more convinced that salvation for farmers lay in efficient methods rather than import duties, and his opinions influenced Acland and Dickinson. When the Somerset Protectionist Society was formed in 1844, neither of them joined, to the great dismay of their supporters. By the time the Irish famine came, and personal letters from friends confirmed the worst horrors of the newspaper reports, Tom felt that he could no longer hold out for Protection, and when the decisive vote was taken in 1846 he and Dickinson went into the lobby for repeal. They both knew that they were committing political suicide, and perhaps some echo of his father's vote on the Reform Bill sounded in Tom's ears. Any lingering hope of continued support from the constituency was disappointed, for at the general election in the following year other candidates were chosen, and both men found themselves out of a job. Tom wrote courageously to his constituents, but it was a hard blow. 'I am sorry to say that when I came to my heap of Parliamentary papers and felt that I was out, it gave me a sick feeling and I turned away from them, having no heart to sort out what is now of no use', he wrote to Mary. So might his father have written in 1832.

The Farmers' Friend

'Don't go to sleep!' said a well-meaning friend, when he heard the news. He need not have feared. Tom's conscience was hard at work, telling him that he owed it to his former constituents to point the way to scientific farming as the surest way to prosperity. But first he must learn more about it himself, and he plunged headlong into a course of lectures on agricultural chemistry at King's College, London. Soon, at Philip Pusey's suggestion, he competed successfully for a prize offered by the Royal Agricultural Society for a Report on Farming in Somerset. His entry—the fruit of several months' hard work spent on farm visits—was a very detailed, methodical study which demonstrated his great powers of analysing problems. He found that Somerset was backward. Apart from the fact that West-Country farmers were proverbially reluctant to take up new ideas, the basic cause was lack of capital investment. While the Corn Laws kept the rents up, there had been little incentive for landlords to spend money, and even if tenants wanted to spend their own, they had no legal right of compensation for their improvements. The results could be seen in wretchedly-equipped farms, unproductive land, and widespread unemployment: even if they were in work, many labourers had near-starvation wages (often paid partly in cider) and miserable cottages. It was true that some local agricultural societies gave awards for long service, and reported 'happy grateful faces', but, as Tom asked, 'what is a coat, buttons and a framed testimonial of merit in return for a life of labour?' He came to the conclusion that Somerset's problems could only be solved by greatly increased capital outlay, introduction of modern methods, and a reform of the law on tenants' rights.

The winning report was published in the Royal Agricultural Society's *Journal* for 1850, and in the summer the Society brought its annual show to Exeter. It was an eye-opener for the West: 'Such a display of gaiety was never before witnessed!' said *Trewman's Flying Post*. The streets were decorated with flags and greenery; the railways gave free transport for beasts and machinery; a huge show yard was set up in the St. Leonards district; trials of horse-hoes, patent ploughs, steam threshing machines and turnip-cutters went on in the surrounding fields. Most of the new implements were to reappear at the Great Exhibition in the following year, under the management of Philip Pusey, and the Exeter Show had almost the air of a dress rehearsal. On the last day, a party went to Killerton by special train, to see Sir Thomas Acland's experimental water-meadows at Newhall Farm, and in the evening M. Soyer, the famous Reform Club chef, prepared a banquet for a thousand people with his new patent gas stoves, in a specially-erected pavilion at the end of Exeter's Queen Street. Tom was tremendously struck with the educational value of such an occasion, and wondered how it could be repeated on a local scale. He decided to approach the Bath and West Society for the Encouragement of Agriculture, Arts, Manufactures and Commerce, which had become moribund after a long and honourable history, suggesting that it should revive its annual show, take it to a different place in Devon and Cornwall every year, and publish its transactions in an instructive journal. The Society was delighted with the idea and took it up with such amazing speed that by April 1851 it was adopted, and preparations began at once for the first annual show, which was to be held in Taunton.

The Widower

The year of the Great Exhibition in Hyde Park and the first Bath and West Show in Somerset was also the terrible year of Tom's bereavement. He and Mary had been eager to bring up their children in the country, but the move to Tetton proved to be a most unlucky one. They were there for less than twelve months before the scarlet fever came, striking down one member of the household after another: by the time three-year-old Cecily died in May, there was only a man-servant who could be spared to take the small coffin to Columb John, and when Mary herself succumbed Tom was almost too ill to take in the news. He and the other children survived, but all his hopes for a happy life seemed in ruins. Sustained though he was by a strong religious faith, he could not conceal his agony of grief. *'Bought when I was a single man to give to some child,'* he scribbled in one of the nursery books, *'now I have children of my own and am a single man again.'*

It was out of the question to remain at Tetton, and Tom took the family to Holnicote, but even there the rooms reminded him of Mary's first visit. The disastrous fire in August hardly seemed to matter. Moving ·into Sprydon did very little to lift his spirits: he tried to give the older children their lessons, and exerted himself to lay out the house and garden for their amusement, but he spent much time in his study, sunk in gloom, and depending heavily on his relations for comfort. Luckily, many of them were within reach, though John Barton was on the point of leaving to found an Acland colony in New Zealand. Tom was fondest of Arthur, the next to him in age. When Tom had drawn back from the Tractarian Movement, Arthur had plunged further in, and was now reckoned to be Dr. Pusey's chief lay friend. Prevented by his tyrannical father from taking holy orders, he had consecrated to the Church, as a layman, all his many talents. They included a knowledge of architecture and astronomy, music, writing, book-binding, and a multitude of crafts. He learned the rudiments of medicine so as to doctor the poor, published several books of prayers and sacred music, and restored a number of churches—sometimes with his own hands. It was typical of him that he was restoring the old chapel at Columb John, and walking back across the fields with his workman's bag over his shoulders, when he received the call to the deathbed of his so-called benefactor, Dr. Troyte,[1] who obliged him to change his name and left him the large derelict property of Huntsham without any funds for its upkeep. This disreputable old 'squarson' had let the church fall into ruins, kept his cock-spurs under the pews, and used his land for sport instead of farming: there were not even any proper roads. Nevertheless, Arthur blessed his name, and he and Fanny, who were rightly regarded as saints by the rest of the family, threw themselves into the task of reclamation. They may have pushed small matters to extremes (no flowers must be picked by the children on Sundays, lest the insects be deprived of their rest), but that did not detract from the utter self-sacrifice with which they turned Huntsham into something like a model estate, complete with a school, parsonage and roads. It was a tragedy that neither of them lived to see the church fully restored.

Leopold, who had been widowed in the same year as Tom, and had three children who matched his in age, was within walking distance at Broadclyst vicarage. He was not such a Puseyite as Arthur; nevertheless, he had taken a theological course at Durham as well as his Oxford degree, held daily services, and lectured on the sacraments in Lent. He modelled himself on Keble, and became priest and friend of every person in the parish. His churchmanship reflected the higher tone which generally prevailed in the Church of England, thanks to the Tractarians. (Even Mr. Stephenson at Selworthy had now been required by his bishop to administer the sacrament six times a year instead of four.)

Farther away, there was always a welcome for Tom in London, at the house of Arthur and Agnes Mills, and also at Oxford, where Henry with his own large brood of children was pursuing his distinguished career. Dr. Acland combined an arduous life as a lecturer and pre-eminent physician with persistent, and ultimately successful, endeavours to win recognition for the study of science at Oxford. A new natural history museum, which he had pioneered with Ruskin's help, was already in prospect, and he was working on the masterly *Memoir on the Cholera in Oxford,* which was to establish him as an authority on public health. A visit to Henry was always a tonic for Tom. Furthest away of any was Tom's youngest brother, John Barton, who, with Charles Tripp, the rector's son from Silverton, was successfully farming 110,000 acres of high sheep-run country in New Zealand, and already in a fair way to achieving his declared aim of reproducing 'the best of England in the Antipodes', with a homestead called Holnicote and trees sent out from Killerton. His visits to England were rare but delightful; Tom pressed him into writing articles on sheep-farming for the Bath and West *Journal,* and the Sprydon children loved the colonial uncle who snatched them away for rides on his saddle and taught them how to make damper-bread on picnic camp fires 'New Zealand style'.

There were also Mary's relations. Chief among them was her first cousin Mary Erskine, who had been like a sister from childhood, and had acted as nurse and comforter of the whole family during the dreadful time at Tetton. The children already knew her as a second mother, for she continued to give Tom advice and help over their upbringing as they grew older. It must have seemed the most natural thing in the world when the two married in July 1856, and the date marked the beginning of a happy partnership which lasted for nearly thirty-six years. Mary Erskine's sweetness and unselfishness shine out of her portrait by Richmond. She must have been very like her cousin and, as it turned out, her qualities were soon tested. Tom's mother died suddenly, five days after the wedding; Mary found that she had a demanding father-in-law on her hands, as well as a husband and five step-children, and, as if this were not enough, the premature deaths of Fanny and Arthur Troyte within 12 months added nine more orphans to the large family circle. A new wing was added to Sprydon and the young Troytes were parcelled out between the three Acland houses in Broadclyst. Mary was a mother to them all.

The Exeter Experiment

At 47, Tom took on a new lease of life (Plates XIIIa and b). During the gloomy years of widowerhood, work for the Bath and West Society had been his best lifeline. The shows had been more and more successful as they travelled around to Plymouth, Tiverton, Bath and Newton Abbot in turn, and there was now a fat annual *Journal,* edited by Tom, which was packed with information on every possible aspect of modern farming. Whether or not he realised that the articles on the 'Prevention of the Incrustation of Steam Boilers', 'The Dentition of Sheep as Indicative of their Age', and 'The Relative Value of Chemical Compounds in Feeding Stuffs and Manures' were rather too difficult for his readers, he became more and more aware of the inadequacy of farmers' education and the need for something better for a coming generation. His old interest in education, which had been lying dormant for a time, was sparked into new life by an article on 'The Education of the Farmer' in the 1856 *Journal,* by Lord Ebrington, the son of his father's old political rival. Lord Ebrington, who had already pioneered a farm-school at West Buckland in North Devon, advocated a complete system of farm-schools and apprentice-colleges, organised on a county basis. Tom, on the contrary, thought that general and not specialised education was needed, and quoted a farmer who had said to him, 'Farmers don't wish to be only farmers—they don't forget that they are men'. To him, the problem was only a part of the predicament which faced the whole of the large, and growing, section of English society which regarded itself as the 'middle' class. There were elementary schools for the labourers, and public schools for what Lord Ebrington called 'the higher ranks', but the middle classes felt left out in the cold. They despised one system, and could not aspire to the other. Although there was certainly a wide choice of private schools, grammar schools and commercial (i.e., mathematical) schools, there was no way of judging their quality except by results, some of which were very poor indeed. There was no common standard.

Tom had always been troubled by the fact that the original proposal for 'middle schools', as part of the great National Society scheme, had never made a start. It now struck him that it was not new schools which were needed, but better standards for the ones which already existed. Why not an independently organised examination open to all comers, of the kind which was used in training colleges? Such a scheme would have great advantages. Nobody would be compelled to enter, there would be no question of government or church interference (both deeply offensive to the independent middle classes), and, above all, no need to spend money on new buildings. Tom no sooner conceived the idea than he decided to try it out in Devon, and he canvassed every school within reach with the zeal and speed which were so much part of his nature. ('Characteristic impetuosity!' said Lord Ebrington, who preferred his own plan.) The response from schoolmasters was enthusiastic; even before a syllabus had been sketched out, more than 100 candidates had been promised. Tom had no difficulty in getting academic friends to set the papers and act as examiners. By the New Year of 1857 a local committee had been formed. In February the Bath and West Society, and—even more important—the government Committee of Council (i.e. Board) of Education, both promised support, and on 17 June 107 candidates came to Exeter to take 'an examination for boys educated in the West of England with a view to employments in Agriculture, Arts, Manufactures and Commerce'. To Tom's special delight, 'two little fellows' from a National Society village school 'walked twenty miles to be there'. A committee of gentlemen who were prepared to put their hands in their own pockets could get things done very quickly in 1857.

'The Exeter Experiment', as it came to be called, was a great success, not only on account of a sensible syllabus which neutralised religious knowledge, or because of the prestigious examiners (Professor Max Müller from Oxford on languages,[2] Professor John Hullah from London on music,[3] and Ruskin himself on art), but also because it proved to be a pilot scheme for something much wider and more permanent.

From the start, the government had put at Tom's disposal Frederick Temple and James Bowstead, H.M. Inspectors of Training Colleges for the Church and the nonconformists respectively. Tom found a lifelong friend in Temple, a man who was 12 years younger than himself and a keen educational reformer whose religious ideas were moving, as were Tom's own, in the liberal direction of the so-called Broad Church. They had never met before, but Temple, the future Archbishop

of Canterbury, was soon writing to Tom, 'You are one of the
very best, if not the best, colleague that I have ever met'. The
examination scheme appealed to him immediately, and he
could not imagine why he had never thought of it himself.
The two men were soon discussing ways of developing it on a
nation-wide scale—as Temple put it, it seemed to grow under
their hands. The great question remained: who would monitor
it? The government and the Church were both ruled out as
certain to be divisive influences. It was a stroke of genius—
perhaps Acland's, perhaps Temple's—which lighted on the
idea of the universities, whose prestige and impartiality were
above criticism. They were sure to win everybody's confidence.
No time was lost in making an approach, and the response
was immediate. 'Exactly what the University ought to do,'
said Cambridge. 'It is wonderful that it should not have been
hit on before,' said Oxford. Matters proceeded at such a pace
that the Exeter Experiment was still in progress when the
University of Oxford began to lay the foundations of its own
local examination system: the examiners were making speeches
of congratulation at a soirée in the Royal Public Rooms in
Exeter on the very day that the University Senate passed the
necessary statute. Cambridge, Durham and Trinity College,
Dublin, soon followed suit, and by the following summer the
first Local University Examinations were being held all over
the country, forerunners of the certificated examinations that
have continued to the present day. In this way Tom's simple
scheme, which had never been meant for anything more than
a local experiment, became ·the examination system which,
under different labels, has ruled secondary education ever
since. Perhaps he would have been disappointed to know how
much of a strait-jacket it has become, and how far his favourite
motto 'Education should be for life, not college' has been
left behind in the struggle for qualifications and status, but,
nevertheless, the Exeter Experiment was his greatest educational achievement and remains his best memorial. In 1858 he
published a pamphlet, *Origins and Objects of the New Oxford
Examinations,* in which he described the whole history of
the project, and in the same year Oxford rewarded him with
an honorary D.C.L.

Feeling that the scheme was now fairly launched, he began to turn his thoughts once more towards Westminster. 'I sometimes sigh for intercourse with the great men of my age,' he wrote in a letter to Gladstone. His old friend gave little hope of a seat at the time. The political kaleidoscope of recent years was at last resolving itself into something like the party system of the present day, with two main forces facing each other across the floor of the House of Commons. Gladstone and Disraeli were the two ascendant stars. Tom's own opinions, however, were still in a state of flux. He called himself 'Liberal-Conservative', but when he went up to Birmingham in 1859, to fight an election against John Bright, the Radical advocate for manhood suffrage, he was very uncomfortable at finding himself at a great public meeting, in opposition to seven or eight thousand working men who were able to answer his arguments point for point. The new intelligent artisan and working classes of the industrial towns were species hitherto quite outside his experience. He lost the election, but he gained a new insight which loosened for ever his ties with the Conservative party. As he said later in the Commons, he learned 'a lesson he would not soon forget'.

The Colonel: a Military Interlude

At this moment, he took up a new 'dog', as Mary called his hobbies. Across the Channel, Napoleon III seemed to be doing his best to emulate his Uncle Napoleon, and the fear of a French invasion swept through England. Volunteer movements sprang up everywhere, and Tom was not behindhand. He determined to rally his neighbouring farmers, and, knowing that they would be most reluctant to assemble merely for foot-drill but would enjoy displaying their horsemanship, he inaugurated the Devon Mounted Rifle Volunteers. They were the first of their kind. The War Office welcomed the idea of infantry soldiers mounted only for the sake of rapid movement —as distinct from the already established cavalry of the Yeomanry—and it spread to other counties: Tom's specially-devised Drilling Instructions were published as an official handbook. At Sprydon, military organisation became the order of the day. For the moment everything else was forgotten in the excitement of deciding on the colour of uniforms, teaching the coachman how to sound the bugle, and devising extra articles of equipment. A cartoon of 'The Overloaded Devon Volunteer' appeared in the national press; a rifle range was set up in the forest (bullets are picked up to this day), with scant regard for safety, and horsemen galloped up and down in front of the house, mounting and dismounting so as to practise hiding in the bushes. Tom became 'Colonel Acland', and grew a beard so as to look the part. Whether or not such furious activity was strictly necessary for the defence of England, it was certainly tremendous fun, and the proceedings had an air of adventure and escape which was reminiscent of Sir Thomas's old carefree days on board the yacht.

This was a great time for the whole family. Tom was much at home, and Mary made an excellent stepmother, who was not too staid to dance reels in holiday-times when the boys came back from school. Charlie and Gilbert were both at Eton; Arthur had gone to Rugby, where Temple was now headmaster. Mary and Agnes, at 14 and eight respectively, had lessons with a governess, watched the Volunteers parading in the drive, and looked forward eagerly to the end of term. They all made the most of the garden, the pond, their numerous pet animals, and the little cottage in the woods, built as a half-serious experiment by their father. Old Sir Thomas would sometimes ride over from Killerton to take them up into the forest on their ponies, and the huge company of cousins added to the fun at Christmas, when Uncle Arthur Mills organised charades, and the traditional ashen faggot was lit in the great hall fireplace. No other house was ever to lay such a spell as did Sprydon on that generation of Aclands.

In due course, the boys went off to college. Charlie's role as a future landowner was already settled, and it was just as much taken for granted that, as the second and third sons, Gib would go into the Army and Arthur into the Church. Tom took special delight in having a soldier-son to whom he could write on martial matters, and—as with all his correspondence—never stinted ink or paper. The government's move to reform the Army and bring the Militia into line, after the disasters of Crimea, gave a special point to their correspondence.

A Liberal

Tom still hankered after more to do, and welcomed the chance to re-enter public life in 1864 when he was appointed to the Schools Inquiry Commission, set up to investigate middle-class schools. His fellow-commissioners included his friend, Frederick Temple, and W. E. Forster, a Liberal M.P., who was to become famous as Gladstone's education minister. Working with them for the three-year period of the Commission broadened Tom's outlook still further. He found himself in sympathy with Temple's contribution to *Essays and Reviews,* a book of liberal theology considered so controversial that it was officially condemned by the Church; and when Bishop Colenso was cold-shouldered because of his modern approach to biblical criticism, Tom took pains to champion him even though high-church friends were upset. ('I am sorely pained,' wrote one clergyman.) His political opinions were changing, too. In 1865, owing to the death of a sitting member, he managed to get himself elected for North Devon, without a contest, as a Liberal-Conservative, but, once he was up at Westminster, the label began to seem less and less appropriate. Contact with Forster had deepened the impression made by the Birmingham election, and when he actually found himself voting alongside his old opponent John Bright for the Second Reform Bill of 1867 he felt that the time had come to call himself an out-and-out Liberal. It meant a fierce fight for his seat at the general election in the following year. He scraped home with a narrow margin, but it was an awkward time for his old supporters, let alone his friends and family. Henry, in particular, was horrified ('How the Electors trust Tom with their votes I cannot tell'), and politics became a permanently divisive issue between the different branches of the family. Old Sir Thomas kept a wise silence. Perhaps he recalled his own disregard for other people's opinions, and saluted the same quality in his son.

The 1868 election brought the Liberals into power with a strong majority, and Gladstone formed his first and greatest ministry. Tom wrote diffidently to his old friend, suggesting himself as education minster, but Gladstone replied with regret that the post was already promised to Forster—a younger man and a Liberal of longer standing. Tom responded with his usual modesty. 'I thought he would have been higher or I would not have written about myself', but he must have understood, for the first time, the full cost to his own political career of his vote for Corn Law repeal so many years ago. He remained a Liberal back-bencher for the next 18 years, and, because he only spoke when he knew his subject thoroughly, he was always listened to with respect from both sides of the House. Education and agriculture took priority, and at the moment there was plenty for him to do in connection with both. Gladstone made him a Church Estate Commissioner, with responsibility for inspecting property all over England, and answering questions about it in parliament. In 1869, when the Endowed Schools Act had carried out some of the Inquiry Commission's recommendations, Tom was made a member of the Select Committee which followed up its work. In the following session, Forster's great Elementary Education Act filled up the gaps in the voluntary system and made primary schooling compulsory throughout the country, and Tom made numerous constructive contributions to the debate: it was a measure of his broadening mind that he could now accept the compromise between Church and State which the Act embodied. Thirty years earlier he had ridiculed the very idea. Now he could truly feel that he was fulfilling his often-expressed ambition to 'be of use', and it was probably just as well that he was not chained more closely to Westminster, for there was more and more to see to at home, now that Sir Thomas was growing so old. It was fortunate that Tom was on the spot when more than half the village of Broadclyst burned down in 1870, so that he could organise the rescue operations. From his bedroom window at Killerton his father watched the distant column of smoke.

The Eleventh Baronet

Sir Thomas died in the following summer. Tom felt proud and half uneasy at being called 'Sir Thomas' up in London. 'It was quite a relief when anyone said "Acland" cheerily in the old way,' he wrote to his wife. Neither of them was in any hurry to leave Sprydon, and Killerton House was shut up for four years, except for the great occasion of May's marriage to Richard Hart-Davis, the Broadclyst curate, in 1872. Gilbert organised an impromptu dance, Tom wept for the loss of a daughter, and everybody was happy. The mood was short-lived. Before the end of the same year 'Gib'—the dashing, delightful lieutenant, who was everyone's favourite—fell ill and died after 20 painful months at Sprydon, nursed by Mary and Agnes. Some of the fun went out of family life for good, and the eventual move to Killerton in 1875 was made with heavy hearts.

Tom, now 62, devoted his main energies for the rest of his life to being a good landlord. It was a role for which he was well equipped, and for once he felt no diffidence. Agnes, the daughter at home, described the new routine:

> At Christmas time, Holnicote for a month. Then Killerton till after Easter, my father going up and down to the House of Commons. He lived a hotel life and came to us for weekends. After Easter, London where we lived in a hired house . . . in the end of July, again to Killerton for August. Then September and half October at Holnicote. Then about a fortnight·at the cottage at Bude. Then Killerton again till Christmas. It was a wandering life, but it meant that my father was on his property.

That was the essential point: unlike his father, who had regarded his tenants as a large, well-loved family who could safely be left—like his own children—to the care of other people, Tom saw them as a school of willing pupils whom he was himself anxious to teach. Throughout life he had an unshakeable confidence in his power to instruct other people in whatever subject lay uppermost in his mind, whether it was art, chemistry, philosophy, or economical cooking, which sat oddly with his genuine modesty, and frequently overwhelmed his friends, who were robbed of any power of reply by his vehement manner. In the present instance, he had a great deal of useful information to impart, and a captive audience: it suited him and his tenants perfectly when he rode round with Mr. Battishill, the chief agent, advising the farmers on the newest methods of cultivation and showing their wives how to make butter. In the same spirit he took over Francis Court, near Killerton, to run as a model home farm, set up a new saw-mill and embarked on a thorough-going programme of much-needed improvement on all the estates, with the help of a family legacy which providentially came from the North Devon branch. He had a sound business sense, which had been denied his father, and at the end of his 27 years' ownership he was able to leave the properties in perfect order and free from debt.

Thanks to the spread of modern methods and 20 years of prosperity, the standard of farming in the 1870s was consider-ably higher than it had been in the days of Tom's prize-winning report, but the old evils of low wages and bad cottages for farm-workers still remained. Broadclyst was better than average. Acland tenant-farmers could afford to pay good money; most of the village had been rebuilt with modern sanitation after the recent fire, and Tom had promoted various schemes of self-help. Even so, when Joseph Arch's[4] new Agricultural Labourers' Union convened a meeting in 1874 'by means of bills headed with a skeleton driving a plough and a stout farmer looking on', it filled the school to overflowing. It was typical of Tom to give them the use of the building and to go to the meeting himself: as *The Times* put it, 'sitting by to hear landowners, farmers, parsons, squires, Church and State generally, Poor Law guardians and even small shopkeepers, well abused for five mortal hours in the presence of the entire village community down to the babe in arms'. It was typical, too, that beneath the tub-thumping rhetoric he found the men 'genial and earnest', and could reply with a good-humoured speech of his own. It earned him rebukes from his fellow-landowners and the Tory Press, but it effectively disarmed the new movement, as far as Broadclyst was concerned. Not that it was Tom's main aim to do so. He was genuinely sympathetic to the labourers' needs, and worried about the best way to help them. They demanded better wages, the opportunity to own some land, and the right to vote. Tom considered that he, as a landowner and practical farmer, already did all he could in the way of giving decent wages and cottages, and that education, thrift and sobriety ought to be able to do the rest. He was very doubtful about giving the vote until these had improved. He was also dubious about the future profitability of farming, which was heading for a decline, as cheap food came pouring in from new developing countries. 'I am sorely puzzled,' he wrote to Gladstone. 'I don't think farmers make great profits, though they live rather luxuriously for their station.'

This could not be said of Tom and Mary who lived as simply as they could. Very little was done to the house or garden at Killerton when they moved in, and Tom even thought of getting rid of the deer in the park: he considered that 'the three Gs—Game, Garden and Gammon' were the worst kinds of extravagance, 'Gammon', or humbug, being understood as anything which he, personally, thought unnecessary. It was essential to renovate Holnicote House, and a couple of rooms were put on to Cloutsham Farm to serve as a holiday retreat; otherwise the Aclands lived simply and spent their money on the estates. Their style of living is described in a book of instructive stories for mothers' meetings called *Ways and Means in a Devonshire Village,* which was dedicated to Tom in 1885, and obviously drawn from life. Like the squire in the book, Tom gave liberal wages to his workmen, and instituted village clubs and reading-rooms, where they could smoke, play bagatelle, or drink coffee, as an alternative to the public house. Like the lady in the book, Mary personally sold her household dripping at half-price to the cottagers and bought comforts for them out of the profits. The cookery lessons wrapped up in the stories ('There should be a pause made after every receipt or practical hint'), include the very same economical dishes of curried cold meat and giblet stew which Tom had learned to make, at sixpence a time, when he attended classes in London especially for the purpose. It could be said, as the Luccombe rector noted after a dinner-party, that the Aclands were 'not a bit grand'.

In the summer of 1879, which was a disastrously wet one for the farmers, a blow fell on the family when Arthur, who had been ordained five years previously and was married, with two little boys, announced his intention of resigning his orders on the eve of stepping into the family living at Luccombe. Tom had failed to heed repeated hints from his son that he was becoming disillusioned with the Established Church, and the news came as an appalling shock. It touched his pride as a leading churchman as well as his religious convictions, and all his tolerance deserted him. He found himself repeating, as parents inevitably must, some of the patterns which had moulded his own childhood, sending letter after letter ('some very severe') to Arthur, and calling on Frederick Temple, who was now Bishop of Exeter, to back up his expostulations. It was all in vain. Arthur had inherited his father's courage to go his own way when his conscience moved him, and the opposition only alienated him from his family. It made a breach that was only partly healed when he made a successful career for himself in Liberal politics, and stood beside his father in the House, six years later.

Since 1874, the Liberals had been out of office, and Tom had to sit on the Opposition benches in the House. Disraeli had come to power on a wave of patriotic sentiment, and foreign policy was parliament's main preoccupation. Social reform, however, was a matter which no party could now afford to ignore, and Tom was able to make useful contributions to debate on a number of progressive measures, including a first Agricultural Holdings Act. The general election of 1880 brought Gladstone back into office, and he immediately invited Tom to make the first speech of the parliament by proposing the election of the Speaker—a formal compliment, which Tom nearly refused, as he had already several times refused a peerage. Honours, he said, were not in his line. Gladstone insisted on making him a privy councillor in 1883, but he was probably much more pleased by the fact that Charlie won a by-election in Cornwall and joined him in the House. As far as Tom was concerned, the most important statutes of Gladstone's second ministry were the Second Agricultural Holdings Act, which put teeth into Disraeli's former measure, and the Third Reform Act of 1884, which gave the vote to rural workers, and redistributed the county divisions. Henceforth, in future, North Devon would only return a single member; Tom decided to move to Wellington, which now included some of the old West Somerset division, and was pleased to find that some of the old farm-labourers had not forgotten his stand against the Corn Laws. He managed to win, with a small majority, and was delighted when, at the same general election of 1885, Charlie got in for Launceston and Arthur for Rotherham. 'Aclands are Trumps!' wrote Gladstone. In the following year, the Liberal party split over the issue of Irish Home Rule. Tom was loyal to Gladstone and narrowly lost his seat. He was frankly disappointed. 'While you are in the fight,' he wrote to his oldest political friend, 'it is a great disappointment to me not to be on the flank or in the reserve.'

There was now more time to spend on his many other interests. In spite of frequent exaggerated references to his own increasing age and failing health ('I am cold and tired, like an old man . . . how one ought to help the feeble aged poor!'), Tom was remarkably fit for his age (Plate XIV). The secretary of the Bath and West Society described him at the shows:[5] 'Clad in a rough home-spun suit with a satchel of agricultural literature for distribution slung low at his side, he would—with some brief spells of rest in the Secretary's office—stride about the Yard all day, with an uprightness of body and elasticity of gait which many a man twenty years younger—for he could thus be seen when he was close upon eighty—might envy.' He was particularly keen on the Show's working dairy, which he had inaugurated himself, and would give impromptu addresses on the subject to any group which gathered round. 'Everybody laughs at me and the dairymaids,' he wrote to his wife; 'I have been getting some tea for the poor girls who are competitors. They are quite exhausted(!).' The home farm became more and more of a hobby, and visitors to Killerton who admired the cream and butter at breakfast might be pressed to walk down the drive and see for themselves how it was made. The steam-plough (still remembered) was another attraction. The Society used the farm for experiments, and trial crops of corn and mangolds grew in the fields which are now bisected by the motorway. In 1940 Jesse Priddle, who had been the shepherd, could still recount how his master, seeing a light in the field from his bedroom window, would come down in the dark, to help with the lambing, getting his frock-coat into a terrible mess, but saying to Jesse as he returned to the house, 'Never mind! I've got people who will see to all that!'

Mary was delighted to have Tom at home, and they revived their old hobby of sketching together, often sitting in the library to put finishing touches or to work up old drawings. She could no longer ride her active little pony, 'The Cat', over the Holnicote hills, but visits to Cloutsham were always the best tonic, and she would conspire with the coachman to drive there ('Cloutsham the Cure!') if Tom seemed depressed. She knew exactly how to manage his variable spirits, lifting them gently when they were down, and bringing common sense and humour to bear when they were too far up: it is hard to imagine anyone who could have done it better. Tom regarded her as more than his intellectual equal—among other things, she could read the Bible in Hebrew—and a rock of emotional strength. Letters, written almost every day when they were apart, show what absolute trust and affection the two had for each other, and with what confidence they could open their minds on every conceivable subject. Mary died in May 1892, and was buried beside the cousin whose work she had taken on so lovingly. Tom was not morbid about the grave, as his father would have been, but he felt the loss just as keenly and knew that an essential part of his life had gone.

He now depended very much upon his children, who often came to stay at Killerton with their families. The small cousins never forgot the nurseries opening on to a balcony which ran up into the hill; the butter for breakfast from the home farm, stamped with a cow; the big wooden bricks which they played with downstairs while the grown-ups ate in the sunny breakfast-room; pony-rides in the park, and picnics in the Bear's House, where tea-things were always kept ready; and the indulgent servants—especially Mr. Garland, the butler, who put posies in the brick-box and allowed them to decorate the dinner-table with scarlet creepers which they pulled off the bushes. Tom was a kind grandfather, who taught them to tie shoe-laces in a special way, came hooting down dark corridors pretending to be an owl, and accompanied his farewell tip of a golden half-sovereign with the remark, 'They'll go and put that in the bank for you I expect, so here's half-a-crown for you to spend yourself!' 'He was a darling and very fond of children,' said one of the little girls, nearly eighty years later.

Charlie often came over from Holnicote where he and Gertie now lived, and took on more and more of the work connected with the family estates. He had retired from parliament on account of poor health, but he found plenty of public work to do in the country, after county councils were established by the Local Government Act of 1888. Arthur, for his part, was a rising man in Liberal politics and in 1892 was made education minister in Gladstone's last ministry, with a seat in the Cabinet. It was the post for which Tom had once hoped, and he rejoiced in it for his son. Cordiality between the two was restored, and a new path at Holnicote was cut and christened 'Cabinet Walk'.

In their last years, Tom and Gladstone—who had kept up a correspondence since their Oxford days—drew more closely together over the questions which they had first discussed at the W.E.G. Essay Society. The great debate between science and religion was now producing a new generation of agnostics, but Tom hoped that Christian belief could transcend the conflict, and in 1896 he published a book, *Knowledge, Duty and Faith*, intended to help young students. He dedicated it to Gladstone, and sent him a copy as soon as it was out, recalling the teaching of Coleridge, who had influenced him so much. Gladstone presented him in turn with a more orthodox religious work of his own.

In 1898 the two men, who had been born within five months of each other, died within 10 days, and Exeter was already in black for Gladstone when the news of Tom's death on 29 May was put up in the post office. Shops were shut in the city, flags came down at the Bath and West Show on the day of the funeral, and nearly three thousand people were crowding the fields round Columb John when the procession reached the end of its journey from Killerton. They had come to mourn a friend.

Chapter Nine

THE RISING GENERATION (1842–1892)

The Brothers

THE TWO BROTHERS who stood by their father's grave were very different. Charlie was 55, and still childless after 20 years of marriage, while Arthur—the younger by six years—had a son, Francis, who would eventually inherit the title and property. It would have been a delicate situation even if the brothers had been congenial, but they had never been on easy terms. It was as if their father's qualities had been split up between them with all the filial piety and love of the estates going to Charlie, and all the adventurous intellect to Arthur. One brother's whole disposition was to conform, while the other's was to question.

Every member of the family had been damaged in some way by the scarlet fever of 1851 which had left them all motherless. Charlie, who had been extremely ill, remained embarrassingly short throughout his life ('Stumps' at Eton and 'Stumpy Jesus' to irreverent villagers in his bearded old age), and in his father's words was never 'thoroughly healthy'—though he managed to row for his Oxford college in four successive seasons. Arthur, on the other hand, escaped the fever, but was far more stunted in personality. He was three when his mother died, and that wound was never healed, in spite of his kind nurse, Minnie, who taught him to love poetry, and remained his friend for life. He always seemed to be the odd man out, partly because of his position in the family (youngest by four years, except for the baby in arms), and partly because of miserable eczema which made him feel like an outcast. The memories of Sprydon, which were so sunny for the others, were tinged with wretchedness for Arthur: he remembered feeling too ashamed of his peeling skin to come in to meals, and going in constant fear of 'being blown up' by his father if he lapsed from the strict religious code of the family. Even calling his sister a 'vagabond' counted as a sin, and he was much afraid of going to hell if he lacked religious faith. It made matters worse when his father remarried in 1856 and he was suddenly told to call his Aunt Mary Erskine by the hitherto sacred name of 'Mama'. His beloved Minnie left to be married in the same year, and he withdrew more and more into himself. To be sure, his elder sister, May, took him under her wing when the big boys went off to school, but in the holidays he felt terribly out of everything. The girls spoke of 'brothers and Arthur' and one of them recalled later that the four of them had run in couples—Charlie and May, Gilbert and Agnes—adding casually 'and Arthur came in somewhere'. He himself felt that he came in nowhere at all. It was little wonder that he grew up full of self-pity, and that to his dying day he harboured the sense that life had made him an exile.

Charlie and Gilbert had no need of self-pity. Charlie drew great comfort from the fact that he was the eldest, and that his father relied on his support. He followed the traditional path to inheritance, through public school, university, the Bar and parliament, with great perserverance, but no particular distinction. His father spoke to Gladstone of his son's 'unobtrusive diligence and good sense', and to these were added great kindness of heart and sincere religious conviction. As for Gilbert, he was a cheerful extrovert who was not afraid of his father, and in consequence got on very well with him. His high spirits made people see him as a throwback to his sporting ancestors, and he even dared to go out with the hounds when hunting was forbidden at home. His short but successful career in the Rifle Brigade suited him exactly: it was very typical of his lively character that he brought back from Canada a black bear, which gave its name to the Bear's Hut at Killerton and was the scourge and delight of the neighbourhood until it was sent to the London zoo.

Holy Orders

Charlie and 'Gib' had both gone to Eton, but when it came to Arthur's turn his father decided on Rugby, out of his regard for Frederick Temple, the new headmaster. Arthur's great asset was a penetrating intelligence, and when he entered the school in 1861 he found exactly the stimulating atmosphere which he needed. Temple was not in the least afraid of innovation. His wide experience of education outside the public-school system was reflected in a novel curriculum which put mathematics, modern languages and natural science on a par with the classics. Moreover, Temple was a progressive thinker as well as an ordained clergyman.

It was a difficult time for the Church. The tide of modern thought was rising in a way that could no longer be ignored, and 1859 had seen the publication of the two most controversial books of the century: Darwin's *Origin of Species,* and the collection of articles entitled *Essays and Reviews,* edited by Benjamin Jowett of Balliol. This work by clerical authors opened up the whole problem of applying contemporary thinking to the doctrines of the Anglican Church. Temple himself had written the first essay on 'The Education of the World', and defended his position to the Rugby governors by saying that the book expressed opinions which badly needed airing. It is hard to realise how courageous this was. Today, most Anglicans acknowledge that Darwin's theory of evolution is reasonable, that every comma in the Bible need not be taken as God's handiwork, and that not every particle of the accumulated doctrine of 2,000 years necessarily expresses the mind of Christ, but in 1859 all these ideas were controversial. To many people they even seemed to threaten the foundation of Christian belief. There was a great outcry, and within a year of publication the authors of both books were attacked so savagely by the Church, in the person of Samuel Wilberforce—Bishop of Oxford and leading prelate of the day—that reasonable dialogue became impossible. Attitudes on both sides hardened. Some churchmen closed their minds to advance, and others turned to an arid Christianity, like Jowett's, which reduced prayer and the sacraments to very little more than superstitions. Many serious people became frankly agnostic.

Eventually many, if not most, of the new ideas were absorbed into the main blood-stream of the Anglican Church, but by that time it was too late: a false antithesis between intellect and religion had taken root in men's minds, and could not be dislodged.

Such was the background to Arthur's school and college days. By the time he entered Christ Church in 1866, the battle-lines in Oxford were firmly drawn up, and Jowett was rapidly establishing Balliol as the centre of intellectual liberalism in the face of strong opposition from Wilberforce and Pusey. Arthur was very little disturbed at this stage. He had always known that he was intended for the Church and that his grandfather wished him to take the family living at Luccombe, near Holnicote. He did not seriously question what he called the 'mild High-churchism' of his upbringing; if anything, it grew more real when he fell in love with Alice Cunningham, the beautiful and devout daughter of the mildly high-church vicar of Witney.[1] After a second-class degree in modern history and law (his family and tutors had expected a first), he returned to Oxford in the autumn of 1870 to attend divinity lectures and prepare for ordination. Almost at once, he was offered an assistant tutorship in history at brand-new Keble College, and accepted with alacrity. Grudging parental approval for courting 'Elsie' Cunningham was received from both families, and life seemed to open up before him. His journal was full of notes for his lectures, comments on his tutorials with undergraduates, and meditations on his theological studies. Every minute of every day was accounted for and apparently enjoyed. The Victorian-Gothic architecture and chapel-worship at Keble gave him the sort of religious background to which he had always been accustomed, but as a young don he had entry into other senior common rooms in the university, and met with many different opinions. He was greatly stimulated: 'I felt I was in a new circle of Gods when I was among first-class men,' he wrote in his journal. Weekends were often spent at Witney, when he and Elsie would walk in the moonlight, go to church together, and discuss the 'prospects' of living at Luccombe. It was settled that they were to be married after he had been ordained a deacon. There was very little recreation otherwise, apart from the traditional Oxford afternoon walk, or an evening at his Uncle Henry's house in Broad Street. He often drove himself too hard, and headaches and depression resulted ('Am I fit to be ordained?'), but he thought that Elsie would solve all his tensions, and worked even harder so as to deserve her. It was a long engagement.

In the early autumn of 1872, after a jolly reading-party with his pupils in the Lake District, he took Elsie on a tour of the West Country where, for the first time, she saw the Aclands in strength. They were a formidable clan: Uncle Arthur and Aunt Agnes Mills at Bude, where there were amusing dinner-parties of cousins, joke telegrams, bathing before breakfast for the men, and the Great September Tide to be watched from the breakwater; Sir Thomas and Lady Acland at Sprydon and Killerton, with newly-married May, and Agnes, still the daughter at home, and finally the whole family assembled together at Holnicote, complete with Gib, newly returned from service overseas, and Charlie, who had been round the world to complete his education and was now at the Bar. Soon they were joined by Uncle Leopold and the family from Broadclyst vicarage. Elsie loyally climbed North Hill after the Sunday service and got wet on Dunkery Beacon, in spite of incipient sciatica. She was justly complimented on her after-dinner singing. Nevertheless, she felt out of it in the huge party. She and Arthur inspected the tiny village of Luccombe, with its very inadequate rectory and school, and grew irritable with each other: she complained of his constant nagging criticism and he accused her of nervousness. The engagement had now gone on for two years, but there were still nearly ten more months, and they were both under great strain.

At Christmas, Arthur was made a deacon, as the first step towards becoming a fully-ordained minister of the Church of England. He was now expected to prepare in good earnest for his priesthood and to carry out many of a clergyman's functions, including preaching in college chapel and lecturing on divinity. He found it an unexpected ordeal. Now that he was obliged to formulate his religious convictions in public, all sorts of previously half-suppressed doubts rose to the surface, with the terrible underlying fear that perhaps he had no real vocation for the priesthood. If only he had been able to open his mind there and then to his father, he might have spared himself and his family much misery. He might well have got a sympathetic hearing, for it was only a few years since Tom Acland had upheld Temple's appointment as Bishop of Exeter, in the face of much die-hard clerical opposition. As it was, the old fear of 'being blown up' prevailed, and he pushed his doubts down deeper, in the hope that they would disappear with prayer, fasting and marriage. Alas, the reverse was the case.

Arthur and Elsie were married in June 1873 and, after a honeymoon abroad, settled down in a little new Oxford villa close to Keble College. Arthur's journal shows the increasing pressure of their life together: illness on her part, overwork on his; more and more time given to preparing lectures and sermons; finer and finer sub-division of the day into allotted tasks; resolutions for getting up earlier never kept, and prayers for 'getting on better with E.' never answered. Finally, he found himself unable to pray or read, and his headaches grew so frequent that he broke down completely. He was forced to give up his tutorship in the spring of 1874 just after his first child, Francis, was born. A year later he was writing in his journal, 'Many things have happened since I last wrote. My work at Keble College is entirely given up. I have to go to Luccombe as Rector within 12 months. My head has been knocked up. I am to give up all pressure of work.' The incident gave him a horror of 'overdoing it' for the rest of his life, and whenever he suffered from headaches or a recurrence of his eczema he was inclined to retreat into invalidism and hypochondria. It was very trying for Elsie, who herself was far from strong, with an ever-increasing tendency to sciatica; at that time she was on the point of giving birth to the second son, Cuthbert, and had spent a good part of her pregnancy in bed. It was a very bad start to the marriage.

Arthur felt far too feeble to protest against proceeding further with ordination as priest, and in any case had been somewhat encouraged in his vocation by the vicar of Sonning, where he had stayed with his sister May. Mr. Pearson called himself 'Broad Church', in the sense of feeling able to accept Anglican teaching as a broad whole, without being unduly disturbed by liberal conceptions of the miracles, the Thirty-Nine Articles, or eternal punishment. Arthur saw no reason why he should not adopt the same position, and under Pearson's guidance took to reading authors like Matthew Arnold, who simplified Christian belief into a system of ethics, and stressed the all-important role of education. In this spirit Arthur went to Yorkshire in April 1875 to work as a curate under his friend Mandell Creighton—a future Bishop of London—as part of his final preparation for ordination as priest. It was not an entire success. In spite of earnest prayers for help, he found it even harder to preach to the villagers of Embleton than to the elite of Keble, and almost impossible to speak convincingly to confirmation classes of young women. He began to feel that the clergy were an utter failure with working people because they were regarded as a race apart. However, he managed to persuade himself that 'half-suppressed doubts were no hindrance', and went forward to his final ordination in July 1875, praying for grace to overcome his difficulties.

By way of a much-needed holiday, he and Elsie now set out on a tour of the north of England, making a careful record of all the beautiful abbeys and cathedrals on their route. The highlight of the whole expedition turned out, unexpectedly, not to be Fountains or Durham, but the grimy cotton town of Rochdale, where years earlier a small group of working men had pioneered the first co-operative store. By now, it had grown into a huge concern, with two large cotton-mills (600 looms in one room, noted Arthur), a large co-operative store and fine libraries, all self-financed. Elsie was just as enthusiastic as Arthur when they were taken on a tour of inspection: best of all, in their eyes, was the Working Men's Club with 900 members, where there was a sing-song every Saturday night, and a political discussion or lecture on Sundays. 'This was our great treat, and we shall not forget our evening there,' recorded Arthur. He suddenly felt in his element: this was what he was born for—an audience to whom he could talk about the things he cared for most, without reserve or dissimulation. In that moment he knew that he could never become a parish priest. It was extremely late in the day to come to such a conclusion, for Luccombe rectory was already being renovated for him, and he had sent down most of his furniture from Oxford. In desperation he threw out hints to his father, persuaded Frederick Hancock, an old pupil, to keep the living warm for him, and escaped with Elsie for a six-months' holiday in Italy, pleading ill-health. There, in Florence, they fell in with T. H. Green[2] and his wife. Green was an old Oxford friend. He had been one of Jowett's pupils, and was now his second-in-command at Balliol, a non-clerical don with an immense influence throughout the university, based on a magnetic personality and unorthodox religious views. He had originally intended to take orders, but had withdrawn because he could not accept the miraculous element of church teaching: his Christian belief was based on the life and teaching of Jesus as a historical figure, and he practised what he preached by helping the poor of Oxford and engaging in local Liberal politics. To Arthur Acland, in his present dilemma, he seemed like a saviour. Arthur grasped eagerly at the idea of a simplified Gospel without an organised Church, and but for his father and step-mother he would have resigned his orders there and then. As it was, he decided that he could bear to continue as a clergyman provided that he did not have to minister or preach, wrote to his family accordingly, and put in for one or two academic jobs when he got back to England in June 1876. By the end of the year he was principal of a new military college at Cowley, just outside Oxford. The place was not a success, and after four terms he left, and established his family in a small house in the city.

However, the time had not been wasted. He gained first-hand experience of classroom teaching, and formed a useful friendship with a colleague, Cyril Ransome, with whom he planned to write a chronological political history of England; his contact with the co-operative movement had prospered during the vacations; he had lectured to the Working Men's Club in Rochdale, and return visits had been made to Oxford by some of its members. He saw a great future for such interchanges. In May 1878 he was appointed secretary of the new University Extension Lectures, and looked forward to the work with eagerness. Visits to Killerton and Holnicote went smoothly, in spite of the decision about Luccombe, and his father talked of raising his allowance and furnishing Allerford as a holiday house for the Oxford vacations. Arthur saw his way ahead to a gentle academic life. By now he had definitely decided to resign his orders, and fully believed that his father was aware of it. There had been a long correspondence with Charlie—who had, unfortunately, taken just the elder-brotherly line which Arthur could least endure—and it was well known that his father, who could never keep anything to himself, had discussed the problem with 'half a dozen bishops and divines of the Church'. It was also widely discussed in Uncle Henry's Broad Street drawing-room. Arthur was therefore quite justified in thinking that he had adequately prepared his family for his final act of resignation in July 1879, and he was amazed when it was received as a bombshell. If he had gone over to Rome or divorced his wife it could hardly have been more of a shock. Not one letter only, but two or three a week came from his father, often 10 or 12 sheets in length, begging him to change his mind. Each was answered, conscientiously and painfully, by Arthur. The arguments for and against were stated and re-stated, misunderstandings explained, stated in a new way, and explained again. Arthur's letters were clear and infinitely courteous, but firm; his father's 'often very severe but kindly meant'. Charlie could not bring himself to write at all, and Arthur could not bring himself even to open Uncle Leopold's envelopes. By October, he was so mentally exhausted that he had to put a temporary stop to the correspondence, by explaining that he was starting a new job as assistant bursar of Christ Church, and writing his history at the same time. Elsie came to his side in this difficult hour. She had never cared for the Aclands in the mass, and she liked them much less now that they were persecuting her husband: it marked a change for the better in the couple's relationship.

In the end, broad-minded Bishop Temple, Arthur's old headmaster, came to the rescue and persuaded Sir Thomas that opposition was unjustified. The final confirmatory document was signed in February 1880, and Arthur was free of his fetters.

Growing Apart

During the next five years the brothers drifted further apart: Arthur chose to feel himself an exile and came seldom to the West, while Charlie settled firmly into his mould as the heir. At the age of 37 it was considered high time that he was married. Ever since travelling around the world—a trip which included a visit to the thriving Acland colony in New Zealand— he had been at the Bar and 'pottering about in society', as Gib put it, without much enjoying himself, and without finding a wife. All his interests lay in the country, and when he did eventually marry in 1879 it was to a close neighbour, Gertrude Walrond of Bradfield. She was one of five beautiful daughters from a family as ancient as the Aclands, with a sixteenth-century manor house near Cullompton, famous for its hospitality. It was considered a splendid match. To be sure, the wedding was a magnificent occasion, and Mary wrote to May of 'beaming faces', but there was an air of formality about it from the start. Gertie, who was tall, graceful and always perfectly dressed, struck her new relations as stiff and grand. She for her part found them too earnest and frugal: she had her own ideas about what was fitting for a future Lady Acland, and they did not include selling dripping to the poor. Charlie, who had always been a little inclined to stand on his dignity— perhaps because of his short stature—was quite ready to fall in with her ideas, and the two settled down in style at Sprydon: the house, which had already been enlarged once to make room for a family of children, was given a grand new wing, and Gertie reorganised the garden.

Charlie now set about becoming an unofficial agent to the family estates. He had always felt at ease among the farmers, and his travels had greatly increased his understanding of their problems. He had seen for himself the sheep-runs of New Zealand, the wheat lands of the Middle West and the cattle-yards of Kentucky, and they had given him a vivid sense of the competition from overseas which now threatened British farming; furthermore, he had been struck by finding farm workers living in much better conditions than any which existed at home. He was able to bring new light to bear on his father's obligations as a landlord, and to enter fully into the educational work of the Bath and West Society, to whose *Journal* he soon became a contributor. National politics were never much to his taste, but it was his duty to get into parliament as a Liberal, and he did so with good grace, becoming member for East Cornwall at a by-election in 1882, just as Gladstone's government was about to start the committee stage of the Second Agricultural Holdings Act, a measure with which Charlie's father was particularly identified. It was a lucky opportunity. Charlie made a number of speeches which demonstrated his common sense and thorough grasp of the subject, and Gladstone, who had already paid him the compliment of inviting him to move the address—the formal start to the session—marked him down for promotion.

So far, Charlie had managed to do all that was expected of him except in one all-important respect: his marriage had produced no children. In an age when the first baby usually appeared within 12 months of a wedding, such a situation soon began to cause concern, not least to Arthur, who had been left next in the line of succession by the death of poor Gib. The last thing in the world he wanted was the ownership of great estates, either for himself or his son. It would run quite counter to the direction in which his own life was developing. 'I shiver when Charlie goes on having no children,' he wrote one Sunday morning, during a visit to Killerton soon after his brother's election victory. The very sound of the chapel bell recalled everything that was part of the Acland tradition ('A.T.', as Agnes called it), from which he now felt wholly separate. 'The place is full of my former self, whom I look at as if a different creature. The huge trees, the big garden, the mass of servants, how grand I once thought all this and seem to dislike it now. I suppose people get gradually sucked into it unconsciously and then cannot throw it off when they have got the comforts etc. around them. What is to be the future of England in the country?' His head was full of Thomas Carlyle's ideas, which the author's recent death and the publication of his *Reminiscences* had brought into particular prominence. They seemed to Arthur like 'his own half-thoughts put into words'. He enjoyed Carlyle's denunciatory style, and especially relished the condemnation of 'gigmanity', a typically obscure term for respectability based on property. It was tempting to think of Charlie as a 'gigman'—not so pleasant perhaps to think of himself or Francis forced into the same role.

In Oxford he was able to take his own line. He went in perpetual fear of another breakdown (there are more references in his journal to his own feelings of being 'seedy' or 'knocked up' than to poor Elsie's frequent bouts of sciatica), but in actual fact he managed to get through an extraordinary amount of work. He was happiest when he was busy. In term-time he and Elsie lived modestly in north Oxford. Every morning he walked or tricycled to work at Christ Church, where he was now the chief administrator, and in addition he coached undergraduates, and interested himself in the affairs of Somerville Hall, the new undenominational college for women. He was their first treasurer ('I have made the garden pay!'), and he gave them history lectures which Elsie was obliged to attend as a chaperone; she confessed later that they had often sent her to sleep. He was also reading voraciously, finding a whole new range of literature now that it was no longer obligatory to look for an Anglican moral on every page. Above all others, he was gripped by Carlyle, whose grand vision of a new unselfseeking political spirit which could transcend the bare rules of economics seemed to Arthur like the very essence of the Co-operative Movement with which he was so much concerned, and he saw himself as the man to spread the message of mutual help and education for the common good. His brilliant extension lectures began to attract packed audiences of co-operators in the North Country; and the Co-operative Congress of 1882, which was held in Oxford at the instigation of himself and his fellow lecturer, Arnold Toynbee, marked the beginning of a much closer partnership between the university and the movement. In consequence, a joint education committee was formed, of which Arthur was made secretary, and an extensive scheme developed which included scholarships at Oxford and a greatly increased programme of lecturing.

During the vacations the pace of life changed. Arthur and Elsie had discovered a delightful little village near Carnarvon in North Wales, and here at Clynnog they built themselves a holiday house on the edge of the sea. In 'this dear place', as Arthur called it, the whole family felt able to relax. The parents took up photography, learned Welsh, and drove through the lanes in a pony-carriage, enjoying the countryside and its people without any pressure from the 'Acland tradition', while Francis and Cuthbert played in the charge of a governess and ran down to the beach at the end of the garden. Clynnog suited everybody's health, which was a most important consideration: Elsie's sciatica or Arthur's headaches were sure to start up as soon as they returned to low-lying Oxford, and even Francis suffered from eczema like his father. The younger boy, Cuthbert, caught scarlet fever in the year of the Oxford Congress and died at seven years old. His death had a fearfully damaging effect on the family. Thanks to his own unhappy childhood, Arthur's personal relationships had never been warm, and he confided to his journal that he could not feel the loss as he should, but Elsie and Francis were inconsolable and poured out their affection on each other in a way that made a possessive, exclusive and permanent bond. Arthur's fatal sense of grievance was stirred, and at home he became more coldly severe and critical than ever. He was inclined to feel that even his own family sided against him.

His temperament was never much of a handicap in his work, which greatly expanded during the next two years. By 1884, the year of Gladstone's Third Reform Bill, he was 'much more saturated in Co-operation than ever before', spending much time in travelling to lectures, committees and conferences as well as working hard to finish a handbook on the movement which he was writing with Benjamin Jones. In Oxford he had become senior bursar of Balliol—a job which included land management—and had collected together a little society of undergraduates known as 'The Inner Ring', which met at his house for supper and political discussion: members included Michael Sadler, J. A. Spender, and Cosmo Lang, the future Archbishop of Canterbury. Arthur found that *certain great principles* in political and social affairs' were becoming more and more clear to him, and it was obvious that his future lay in a parliamentary career. Letters of invitation began to come in from constituencies where he was already well known as a speaker; his father gave hesitant approval ('would his health stand it?'), and in July 1885 he was adopted as prospective Liberal candidate for the newly-formed division of Rotherham. He must have felt that all the work of the preceding five years had been apprenticeship for this, his true vocation.

Aclands are Trumps

The general election of 1885, fought on the new extended franchise, was a family affair. Tom went to speak for both his sons ('one of the greatest pleasures of my life,' wrote Arthur), and there were great rejoicings at Killerton when all three men topped the polls. 'We had 20 telegrams yesterday! The Broad-clyst men walked backwards and forwards all day!' reported Mary in high delight, and when the new parliament met in January there was no prouder man in the House of Commons than Sir Thomas Acland.

Charlie's patience and industry on the back-benches were rewarded by Gladstone, who made him under-secretary to the Board of Trade and Parliamentary Church Commissioner—jobs which chiefly entailed answering a multitude of questions in the House—while Arthur, the newcomer, learned his way around Westminster and made friends with other young Radicals. However, Gladstone's ministry only lasted for four months before the Liberal party split over the issue of Irish Home Rule. In the general election which followed, Charlie and Arthur kept their seats, but Tom and many other Home Rulers lost, and, when parliament reassembled, the Liberal Unionists (who opposed the idea of Irish independence), shifted away from Gladstone into the arms of the Conserva-tives opposite, leaving their old leader and his Home Rule Liberals in a thorough minority. For the next five years the country was ruled by Lord Salisbury's Conservative-Unionist government which concentrated on coercing Ireland into obedience and on cutting a figure abroad, while a programme of uncontroversial domestic reform rolled through parliament almost unopposed. The Acland brothers sat on the opposition benches, on easier terms with each other again, though the difference between them was more marked than ever. Charlie was a conscientious member for North-East Cornwall, who made short practical speeches whenever the occasion demanded, like the short practical man that he was; he was always thankful when the session ended and he was able to go back to the West Country. Arthur, on the other hand, relished his new life and, under the elder statesmanship of John Morley, became one of the group of younger Liberals—including Haldane, Asquith and Grey—who would one day lead the party. The new franchise had brought a few working men such as Joseph Arch into parliament, and these forerunners of the Labour party regarded Arthur Acland as their special ally. Influenced by them, he began to develop the vision of an ideal society based on the co-operative principle of self-help, and he looked forward to a day when townspeople would enjoy good wages, free libraries, public baths and clean streets, by the exercise of their own self-government, while villagers would own their cottages and land, and organise parish life quite independently of the squire or the parson. The key to it all must be better education, and it was to this cause that he now devoted all his energies.

Away from parliament he divided his time between lecturing for the extension and co-operative movements, keeping contact with the 'Inner Ring' and getting to know the pitmen and iron-workers of Rotherham, where he founded the 86 Club for education in citizens' duties: 'This is the best thing I can do. Read and work for this', he wrote in his journal, during his first summer recess. Presently, new friendships with Liberal members from other industrial towns opened his eyes to the great needs which existed, apart from adult education. Elementary schooling was by this time compulsory but not free, with the result that attendance was still poor and prosecutions were frequent. Beyond the age of 11 there was nothing for clever children except the miscellany of endowed and private schools which Arthur's father had worked so hard to unify, and these only catered for a fraction of those who could have benefited. Worst of all, for a country which led the world in industry, was the crying need for more instruction in science and practical art. The Department of Science and Art (a legacy of the Great Exhibition) gave haphazard grants to establishments which professed to teach these subjects, but it was entirely separate from the Board of Education. The result, according to John Morley who in 1888 seconded a resolution of Arthur's on secondary and technical education, was that 'everything in our education system between the elementary schools and the Universities was in a state of neither more nor less than chaos'. It had always been difficult to stir up enthusiasm for secondary education in England because the legislating classes could afford to send their own sons to public schools, and considered that there was very little wrong with things as they were. They were particularly apathetic about technical education because, on the whole, they despised trade. In the rest of Great Britain the situation was different. In Wales especially, where there were hardly any endowments and no public schools, there was a keen desire to get a proper system organised. The first effective thrust for reform came from the Welsh members of parliament who were too poor to send their children away to England, and in 1889—the year after the Local Government Act which created the county councils—a Private Members' Bill for Welsh intermediate (i.e., secondary and technical) education managed to pass through parliament. It provided for education committees, composed jointly of councillors and government nominees, to be set up by each Welsh county council to work out a scheme in detail. Money was to be raised by local rates, augmented by the Treasury.

It was a stroke of luck for Arthur. He had already been made an alderman of Carnarvon County Council by virtue of his residence at Clynnog, and when the new Joint Education Committee was formed he was the natural choice as its chairman. It was one of the most memorable days of his life when, as he recorded in his journal, 'the first meeting of the first Committee ever assembled to start organised secondary education in Great Britain' met on 8 November 1889. His appointment as chairman was apt. Not only was he exceptionally well-equipped as an educationalist and an administrator, but he was also thoroughly imbued with the spirit of the Welsh Revival which had been the motive force behind the Bill. Soon after entering the House he had struck up an acquaintance with the young Liberal member for Merioneth, which was to become the

closest friendship of his life. Tom Ellis was the son of a small
Welsh farmer who had fought his way to Oxford, and saw himself as the future leader of an independent Wales; with his
idealism and total absence of 'gigmanity' he was an ideal
companion for Arthur. He was often a guest at Clynnog, which
was now the Aclands' main home, and he taught them to see
Wales through his own eyes, not merely as a beautiful holiday
retreat, but as a freedom-loving nation of Welsh-speaking,
chapel-going Liberals tyrannised over by an occupying power
of Anglican landlords and clergy intent on imposing their own
English culture. It was a view which appealed strongly to
Arthur's nonconformist disposition. His star was now in the
ascendant. He had found, as he said, a 'pivot' for his work in
Welsh education, and now he never seemed to 'overdo' or
'feel seedy', however much he did. He was an excellent
administrator, with the power of making other people enthusiastic; the new Education Committee worked so hard and well
under his chairmanship that within 12 months a complete
scheme for intermediate education had been drafted and put
before the county council, making Carnarvon the pace-setter
for the rest of Wales. He also inaugurated and presided over a
standing conference of all the Intermediate Committees, which
eventually became the Welsh Central Board of Education.

During this same lucky year of 1890, he greatly increased
his stature in the Commons. Just before the opening of the
new session in February John Morley and 'The Brethren', as
he called his group of young Radicals, discovered that there
was to be no mention of education in the inaugural Queen's
Speech, and asked Arthur to move an amendment on the
point. Arthur rose to the occasion and, after a week's hard
preparation, made a 50-minute speech calling for free elementary schooling, which demonstrated his powers of wit and
absolute mastery of his subject. There was cheering when
he sat down and his amendment was only narrowly beaten:
he considered it the best speech he had yet made. The Easter
recess was entirely given over to electioneering by both the
Aclands. A by-election occurred in Carvarvon Boroughs and
David Lloyd George, then a 27-year-old solicitor, who was too
poor to pay a political agent, stood as the Liberal candidate.

'It was a fight of a young untried man of humble birth against all the powers of land and Tory wealth,' wrote Arthur, who organised the whole campaign and thoroughly enjoyed the chance of denouncing the Established Church and English 'gigmanity' from the platform, while Elsie enthralled audiences by singing 'Land of My Fathers' in Welsh. It was a moment of great triumph when their candidate won by 18 votes and was drawn through the streets of Carnarvon to cries of 'Three Cheers for the boy M.P.!'. '. . . a dogmatic fellow without much tact, and I don't know how he will do in the long run', commented Arthur after presenting the new member to the House. There was one more triumph before the summer recess. The government had decided to put down drinking by increasing taxation and reducing the number of public houses. Some of the money was to be earmarked for compensating redundant licensees, but Arthur managed to move an amendment which had the effect of diverting this 'whiskey money' into education, to be spent at the discretion of county councils. It made a substantial addition to the Welsh Act's budget, and he was particularly proud of having defeated vested interests and benefited his own cause at one blow.

He went back to Clynnog tired but exhilarated and enjoyed a thorough holiday with Elsie in North Wales before turning again to his committee work. He felt unusually well, and so did Elsie: she had managed to spend some of the session in London, listening to Arthur's speeches from the gallery, and going to the theatre with him, and her sciatica seemed to be in abeyance, though she was careful to spend regular periods at Matlock or Buxton, having 'spa' treatment. She and Arthur were in their early forties and were beginning to enjoy life, perhaps for the first time. However, the easing of tension had an unexpected effect: like a thunderbolt came the news that Elsie was pregnant—at the age of forty-two.

Cabinet Walk

The upset came at an awkward moment for everybody. Elsie's heath was always precarious: she had been told long ago to have no more children, and there was a nervous element in her perpetual retreats into illness which augured badly for another confinement in middle life. Arthur decided to leave Clynnog, in order to be near good doctors, and picked on Scarborough, partly on account of its supposedly healthy air; but the last thing he wanted was extra expense and worry just when he was beginning to taste the fruits of success. He felt short of money as it was. His father allowed him £1,000 a year, and paid for Francis's education at Rugby, but Arthur felt that it was not enough. Here was he, a rising man in politics and sure of office if his party came to power, while Charlie was a nobody, who was about to leave parliament altogether because of weak health. Furthermore, it was quite clear by now that Charlie would have no children, and Arthur grudged the fact that he was bringing up his brother's heir. He did not approve of patrimony on principle—it went clean against his ideas of a property-owning democracy—and, at a deeper level than he was aware of, there lay his old childish emotion of wanting more for himself.

All this came out in a conversation between the brothers, and was anxiously conveyed by Charlie to his father. They were both perplexed. No cash was immediately available, and it was a point of honour to keep the land intact. By contrast, Arthur would cheerfully have sold off whatever was required to give him an adequate income, but his father had no idea of this. In perfect innocence, Sir Thomas hit upon the plan of giving him Loxbeare, a small family property near Tiverton, which yielded about £500 a year, with a half-formed idea of linking him to the West Country. Arthur was horrified. He was anxious not to upset his father, but he felt bound to point out that all his interests lay in the north of England, and that if he were given Loxbeare he would certainly sell it. The idea was soon dropped. Somehow his allowance was raised to £1,500— enough to provide him with a house in London as well as one in Scarborough, an annual holiday abroad, and unlimited medical attention for Elsie—but he still felt pinched, and blamed his brother for not getting him more.

As for the wives, they were poles apart. Elsie's principles of 'plain living and high thinking', her keen interest in politics, and her preference for picturesque 'Liberty' garments over the nipped-in fashions of the day were in direct contrast to the tastes of her elegant sister-in-law, and in the words of a later generation the two women conducted a 'polite civil war'. Francis, who was now a handsome schoolboy, taller than his parents, acted as an awkward go-between. His uncle and aunt frequently invited him to stay, and he acknowledged their real kindness, but he was also well aware of his parents' feelings, and felt duty-bound to refuse tips of money at the end of the holidays. Like his father, he felt great misgivings about the prospect of a new addition to the family.

Mabel Alice, born on 17 April 1891, was reported to be 'very healthy though small', and Elsie pulled through a difficult confinement and a subsequent operation with the help of London doctors. The healthy air of Scarborough helped her convalescence, and by June of the following year she was back in full health and helping her husband in the general election campaign at Rotherham: she proved so successful as a speaker that he was able to leave her in charge for eight days while he went on a tour of other constituencies. 'Elsie did wonders on my behalf, speaking to half-a-dozen meetings and to a special women's meeting and singing. She must have helped *enormously* to keep up the enthusiasm,' he wrote in his journal, when he recorded an excellent victory at the polls. The result of the election, nationally, was a narrow win for the Liberals, and Gladstone formed his last ministry with a majority of only 43, which included the Irish members. There was thus no clear mandate for anything except Irish Home Rule. Much speculation went on within the small group of younger Radicals about the chances of office. Arthur's own reputation was high. Haldane wrote to the Chief Whip:[3]

> I am convinced that the man in our ranks who possesses, beyond anyone else of his standing, the confidence of the labour party, using the term in its widest sense, is Arthur Acland. He has, as none of us younger man has, the personal respect of not only prominent leaders like Tom Mann and Burns, but' of the great body of artisans of the northern and midland counties. He is looked on by them, and I think rightly, as having done more really good work in the House of Commons in the last five sessions than any other member of his standing. Besides this, he is regarded by the Welsh members as one of themselves, because of the services he

> had rendered them in intermediate education and other matters, . . .
> He is in a unique position.

Arthur had thought of himself as a whip, or perhaps in charge of a Labour department of the Board of Trade, but he was quite unprepared for the offer which came. 'It is all over. I have not yet recovered my breath,' he wrote in his journal on 26 August 1892: '—a man was bringing a letter which I opened on the stairs, just below the door of our flat—I saw in a moment almost "Education Office—with a seat in the Cabinet" in the G.O.M.'s admirably worded letter . . . E. and I gasped, as some of the world will gasp.' He was tremendously elated. The new Cabinet, which included Asquith as Home Secretary, and Grey as Under-Secretary for Foreign Affairs, travelled down to Osborne, steaming into Cowes as the old Cabinet steamed out, and shuffled around on their knees in frock coats to take the oath and kiss the Queen's hand. There was a good deal of pleasant chaff about the antiquated ceremony on the way home. Back in London, Arthur found it most exhilarating to attend his first Cabinet meeting, explore his new office in Whitehall, and to be seen off at the station by a messenger with a red box. After a triumphant reception at Rotherham and a brief visit to Holnicote ('C. quite the monarch and G. far away'), he and Elsie set off for a holiday in the Alps with Tom Ellis. It was 'a glorious time with our carriage, singing and much fun—splendid weather—the scenery most beautiful!' he wrote, in a rare surge of high spirits, almost worthy of his ancestors.

By October, the Aclands were settling into their new house in Cheyne Walk, next door to J. A. Spender, the editor of the *Westminster Gazette,* and close to Tom Ellis, who lived in Oakley Street. The next three years were to be by far the most strenuous in Arthur's life, and it must have been the sheer excitement of his work which carried him through without a breakdown. It was quite otherwise for poor Elsie, who felt neglected and lonely, and was seldom well enough even to visit the Ladies' Gallery to listen to her husband's speeches. She soon succumbed to a series of unexplained illnesses and ineffectual surgical operations which made London life impossible for her. Arthur was intermittently anxious, but he afterwards admitted that he never had any idea of how depressed she had been during his years in office. He himself faced his future with confidence. The cumbrous old title of 'Vice-President of the Committee of Council on Education' still clung to his office, but he had the great advantage over all his predecessors of a seat in the Cabinet. He also had great personal assets, for he possessed, in a unique combination, the qualities of a first-rate administrator, an experienced educationalist, and a red-hot social reformer. Even the characteristics which sometimes made him an awkward husband and father served him well, and his new job often benefited from his severe critical faculties and his conviction that he was in the right. A cutting edge was a great advantage in parliamentary debate.

Among his friends and colleagues, his personality blossomed as never before, and he was more at ease, socially, than at any other time in his life. On account of Elsie's absence he did not frequent the drawing-rooms of fashionable political hostesses, but his position as Cabinet Minister carried with it a social life of its own for which he was far better fitted. 'I sit on the front bench as if I were born to it. I find my private room invaluable . . . I stick *very tight* to the House—have dined with the Prince of Wales—been to levee etc.', he wrote soon after the start of the session in March 1893. For the first time in his life, he felt that he was properly valued; there was no taint of 'gigmanity' about a position that had been so truly earned. The little private room became the scene of frequent dinners with Asquith and Morley, so full of wit and sparkle that Morley begged him to continue ('the only half-hour in the day he enjoyed'); friendship with Spender and his assistant-editor-cartoonist, F. C. Gould, kept his name and face in the pages of the *Westminster Gazette* (Plate XVb), and he walked back to Chelsea every night with Tom Ellis, the Assistant Whip, feeling that he was in the swim at last.

With such a shaky majority in the Commons, an aged leader who cared for nothing but Irish Home Rule, and an exceptionally obdurate House of Lords, it was no time to embark on the reform of secondary education, and Arthur contented himself with writing a memorandum on the subject, meanwhile watching

with satisfaction as his Welsh Intermediate Scheme came to
fruition and provided the rest of the kingdom with an object-
lesson. At the same time, he stirred up his Whitehall department
by injecting some badly-needed new blood, and instituted a
new Departmental Committee with the Charity Commissioners
and the Department of Science and Art, foreshadowing a single
central authority for education.

As for elementary schooling, it was no longer much of a
party question, although there were still important differences
of opinion about how it should be paid for. The most divisive
issue was the 'religious question'. Since the Education Act of
1870 the voluntary church and chapel schools had managed
to run in tandem with the state-run Board schools without
too much friction, but the recent introduction of free education, in a belated measure of Salisbury's government, had put
them into financial difficulties. They received substantial
grants from the State, but—unlike the Board schools—got
nothing from local rates. Voluntary subscriptions did not make
up the difference, and now they were not even supposed to
charge 'school pence'. Some of the schools, especially in poor
country districts, were already in a disgraceful state, and
standards were falling further and further behind. Arthur, who
had no love for church schools, determined to bring them to
heel by means of the Department's annual Codes, the quasi-legal
regulations by which the payment of grants was governed. His
first Code, which made it plain that no grants would be made
to schools which were not roomy, warm, ventilated, and
supplied with sanitary accommodation, threw many churchmen
into a frenzy of protest. There were still backwoodsmen in both
Houses of Parliament who considered that elementary schooling
was well enough served if the largest possible number of
children were crowded into the smallest possible space at
minimum expense provided that they learned the creed and
catechism, and such men bombarded Arthur with accusations
of being a 'faddist' for demanding such rudimentary facilities
as cloakrooms and playgrounds. He was on his feet nearly every
afternoon at Question Time, answering their complaints with
admirable fairness, and only permitting himself to be bitter
when he was personally attacked: for example, when it transpired

that Lord Salisbury had made a special trip to Holnicote to discredit Arthur by showing that he favoured his father's schools at Luccombe and Allerford—an attempt which fell flat when it turned out that his lordship had left one of the buildings with the audible comment that 'it was too good for his purposes'. Fortunately, the majority of reasonable churchmen agreed with the Bishop of Rochester, who said in the House of Lords, 'If we are to go on receiving grants for our schools, it seems fair and right . . . that we should be compelled to meet modern requirements', and in most cases, enough money was found. Although future Conservative governments were to be more lenient, an important principle had been established.

During the marathon session of 1893-4, which stretched into the spring with hardly a break for Christmas, Gladstone's Ministry fought with its back to the wall for Home Rule and Local Goverment Reform, only to be frustrated by the Lords, who threw out one Bill and mangled the other. In March, the Grand Old Man resigned in disgust, and was succeeded by Lord Rosebery, who presided over an unhappy, jealous Cabinet for a further year of insecure Liberal rule. Arthur, whose own position was well established, was not disturbed by the bickering of his colleagues and, as he wrote to 'his father, it was something of a relief to have proper Cabinet meetings at a long table, instead of being obliged to gather round Gladstone in a double ring because of his deafness. Without the continual strain of late-night sittings he was better able to concentrate on administrative work, and 1894 saw some of his most important achievements. The most far-reaching was the setting up in January of the Royal Commission on Secondary Education under James Bryce, which was to lay the foundations of Balfour's Education Act of 1902, and it was typical of his interest in women's education, which had begun with his lectures to the Oxford ladies, that three of the 16 Commissioners were women. At the same time, he was using the Department's Codes to liberalise the elementary school curriculum by abolishing the farcical 'payment by results'— whereby grants were earned by teaching children to repeat the three Rs like parrots,—and introducing new grant-earning subjects such as cookery, handicrafts, physical education, and visits to museums and art galleries, on the (apparently) novel principle that children learned best when they enjoyed what they were doing. The school-leaving age was legally fixed at 11; a 10-minute break after every two hours of lesssons was made compulsory, and parents were encouraged to press for the right to free schooling. In addition, a non-controversial Bill to help blind and deaf children was slipped through parliament in a pioneer attempt to provide special education for the handicapped.

By the spring of 1895 Arthur was beginning to feel worn out, and the danger-signals of eczema, breathlessness, head-aches, sleeplessness, and inability to concentrate warned him of imminent collapse. His last constructive effort was to set up a new Office of Special Enquiries within the Education Department, to carry out research, under the direction of Michael Sadler, a brilliant ex-member of the Inner Ring—a bold and original scheme which foundered because of personal difficulties within the Department, but which, nevertheless, provided an invaluable body of information for future adminis-trators. Nothing like it was attempted again until 1961.

Arthur began to complain of the incessant pressure of speech-making at official functions, obligatory visits to Windsor and Sandringham, and innumerable school foundation-stone ceremonies, and to say that he would be glad to be out of office. When the government fell, in June 1895, it was a positive relief. He was 'utterly squeezed out' all the autumn, spoke of 'brain collapse complete', and felt as if he needed a year or two of continuous life in the country to get back his strength. When he looked back over the three years and reflected upon how much he had got done, in Session and out, he was simply amazed. As he wrote in his beloved journal: 'At any rate some good things for the country were done in 1892–5 in legislation and administration. But it was a queer bustle, and a wonder that we got through so well.'

Chapter Ten

THE LAST PATRIARCH (1898-1917)

Head of the Family (Plate XV a)

BY THE TIME HIS FATHER died in 1898 Arthur had decided to resign his seat in parliament after three years on the Opposition front bench spent in fighting, with success, to prevent the Conservative government from undoing all his good work in the Education Department. There must have been an element of hypochondria in his conviction that to go on any longer would mean 'brain collapse complete', for he lived for another 27 years in reasonably good health, apart from his chronic allergic complaints, and he made some notable contributions to the causes he cared for. Nevertheless, he was right in thinking that his main achievements lay behind him. His brother's were still to come.

Charles Thomas Dyke Acland was more than ready to take his place as the 12th holder of the family title, and very anxious to live up to his inheritance. There was now a second baronetcy in Oxford, Doctor Henry having been honoured by Queen Victoria for his signal services to medicine, and Charlie was determined that the two should not be confused. He therefore gave out that he wished to be known as 'Sir Thomas', explaining that otherwise people might not know 'which was the real head and owner of Killerton'. The action irritated the illustrious Oxford branch, and amused Arthur and Elsie, but caused no surprise in Devon. There had been a Sir Thomas Acland at Killerton for 170 years and any other name would have seemed like a break with tradition. As Arthur had always maintained, Charlie's mind was essentially feudal.

Since the days of the 'Peak of Prosperity' the family estates had somewhat shrunk, thanks to marriage dowries, expensive

elections, and the excessively open-handed ways of the Great
Sir Thomas, but they were still wide enough to make Charlie
the second largest landowner in Somerset, with 16,000 acres,
and among the top 10 in Devon, with 15,000 acres. He also
owned 5,000 acres in Cornwall. It was typical of his temperament that his first concern was to make Killerton into a suitable
capital for such an important empire. He and Gertie considered
that the house was thoroughly old-fashioned. Unlike Bradfield
or Huntsham Court—where another Walrond daughter, married
to Charles Troyte, was living and had virtually rebuilt the
house—Killerton had escaped alterations during Victoria's reign.
There was no heating except for open fires, and no lighting
apart from candles and oil, while the sanitary arrangements
were still very much as they had been in 1811 when the house-
carpenter recorded his hours spent on remedying 'the stench in
Sir Thomas's water-closet'. Apart from these mundane considerations, the Aclands wanted a house where they could
entertain on a grand scale. House-parties were the fashion,
and Gertie longed for a large drawing-room and a living-hall
with a staircase leading down into it, where guests could gather
round the fire before dinner and watch the ladies descending
in their finery. Charlie wanted a billiard-room where the men
could smoke without being turned out into the garden orangery,
and also a better place for estate business than his grandfather's
old 'justice room' upstairs. They must have been planning the
alterations for years: it was only three months after his father
died when Charlie summoned Mr. Prothero, an architect from
Cheltenham, and gave him precise instructions. By December
sketch-plans had been approved, and within two years the
Aclands moved into Killerton House, completely rejuvenated,
at the cost of over £8,000.

The original architect, John Johnson, would scarcely have
recognised it. His modest pediment-crowned entrance had been
abandoned for a new and awkward porch which stuck out at
the side of the house on to a broad gravel carriage sweep with a
handsome new single-storey billiard-room on the further side,
and the bedroom windows had all been enlarged—some people
thought to the detriment of their proportions. Inside, the
changes were even greater. Gertie's grand drawing-room had

been achieved by throwing the previous entrance-lobby and morning-room into one, with showy sham-marble pillars instead of a dividing wall, and the old dining-room had become a living-hall by means of a ruthless reconstruction involving an impressively heavy new oak staircase with an archway opening it up to view from below. Heat was supplied by a great boiler in the cellar, feeding bulky radiators hidden behind ornamental metalwork, and electricity was installed throughout the house, with an accumulator-room opening on to the back yard and a switchboard in the hall, which nobody except the estate foreman could understand. Johnson's plain ceilings were embellished with mouldings in Adams style and, as the crowning touch, Charlie and Gertie had their portraits in plaster added to the decorations in the dining-room. They now felt that, at last, they had a country seat worthy of their position; Gertie could invite her large parties to stay, and Charlie could sit at the study end of the new billiard-room with its own 'steward's entrance', and conduct the affairs of the estate with proper dignity.

Landed Property

It was the general opinion that the new Sir Thomas made a splendid landlord, Now that he was securely in command, the diligence and common sense, which were his best qualities, showed themselves to great advantage, and his intimate knowledge of the estates, accumulated over a 20-year period as his father's understudy, stood him in excellent stead. However, he had none of the impulsive energy which had taken his father on impromptu expeditions into the park at night to help the shepherd with the lambing. His style recalled that of his old grandfather and, as a cousin remembered, 'he had rather a patriarchal appearance and attitude towards his tenants and lesser members of his family'. He took the keenest possible interest in the management of his property, but it was so large and so scattered that he was bound to depend, as his forebears had done, on the help of agents and stewards. First in line came Mr. Battishill, the senior partner in a firm of Exeter solicitors which had looked after the Aclands' affairs for a number of years. He combined the roles of a present-day land-agent and a confidential family man of business. His position lay somewhere between friend and professional adviser: he was on easy enough terms to carry his gun at a shooting-party or take his place at the dinner-table, but he would never have dreamed of addressing Charles in anything but the most formal way. He knew all there was to know about the family's financial affairs, and well understood the delicate problem of the inheritance. He himself had advised the late Sir Thomas to leave his property in such a way that Arthur could never sell any of the land, but, when he realised that Arthur's grievances over the will were amounting almost to monomania, he persuaded Charlie to allow his brother some extra cash, and so brought about a temporary truce. Great diplomacy and discretion were demanded of Mr. Battishill.

The 'agent', as he was called, kept overall control, and dealt with such important questions as farm-tenancy agreements and major improvements, but everyday management was left to sub-agents known as stewards—Mr. Stevens at Killerton, and Mr. Birmingham at Holnicote—who, in their turn, were accountable to the agent for a considerable body of estate workers. Mr. Stevens, who looked after Killerton, the north Devon estates and Trerice and Bude in Cornwall, lived at Budlake with a small estate office attached to his house. Quite apart from the outlying properties, which had bailiffs or clerks-of-work on the spot, he had the management of the home farm with eight men, the stables with a coachman and two grooms, the forest and park with two woodmen, two gamekeepers and a trapper, and the estate yard with 13 building workers. All the men were paid on Thursdays from piles of coins stacked ready for them on Mr. Stevens's desk. There were very few gold sovereigns in the weekly piles, for the average man's wage was 1s. 8d. a day, and even the coachman and estate foreman earned little more than 4s. a day. With the 13 gardeners, who came under the jurisdiction of a head gardener, the total wages bill for 45 men only came to £30 a week. Mr. Birmingham managed the two Somerset properties of Holnicote and Winsford on similar lines, and, for all this responsibility, each steward was rewarded with £140 a year as well as a house and some comfortable perquisites. The whole great self-regulating network resembled, as it had done for centuries, an extended family with a patriarch at its head, and, for the security of that relationship, employees were prepared to accept low wages and give a lifetime's service in return.

The main revenue of the estates came from farm rents, which were paid twice a year, at Lady Day and Michaelmas, in eight separate places: Killerton, Loxbeare, north Devon (two places), Holnicote, Winsford, Trerice, and Bude. The procedure was the same everywhere. Mr. Battishill would arrive from Exeter with a senior clerk, and Mr. Stevens or Mr. Birmingham would meet him at some convenient place. In Broadclyst it was the Institute and Reading Room built by the late Sir Thomas. The 30 farm tenants would appear during the morning, dressed in their best, and enter one by one while the others stood outside and compared the state of their crops. This audit was always held on the day after Cullompton Fair, so that the farmers could have the best chance of selling their produce and getting some cash to pay their rents. Inside, the clerk and Mr. Stevens would be sitting at a table in the first room, where the rent was paid and small accounts and queries settled. Mr. Battishill sat in the further room, where more serious matters could be brought up and strong words spoken if necessary: it was a great time for complaints on both sides. At the end of the audit a dinner was held in the *Red Lion,* the agent and steward presiding, at which toasts were drunk and speeches made. Mr. Battishill might well read a letter from Sir Thomas or address the tenants on some unpopular topic, such as the impossibility of reducing the rents, but the day's business always ended in a civilised and friendly way. In due course Mr. Battishill would convey the outcome to Sir Thomas. These were bad times for farming, even on the rich Killerton land, and on the hill-farms in north Devon and Somerset the situation was almost desperate. In 1900 all the tenants at Holnicote and Winsford complained of low wool prices and scarcity of labour, and asked for reductions in rent. There were fewer complaints at Trerice, but Battishill 'saw signs of money wanting'; Bude, which was becoming a fairly popular seaside resort, was waiting for the railway and a gas-works to bring it prosperity. Even at Killerton there were defaulters that year ('must have a firm hand kept on them'), and a certain tenant was farming so badly that he deserved to be given notice to quit. 'He will probably call at Killerton!' warned Battishill. We may be sure that he did so and that he received a courteous welcome. It was a great merit of the system that if any tenant had a complaint he could go straight to his landlord, who was the final arbiter. Even if the tenant failed to gain his point—and Charlie rarely disagreed with his advisers—he felt that he had gained a fair hearing and was satisfied.

Charlie was very conscious of the importance of keeping a personal relationship with his tenants, and aware that it was much more difficult to do so on outlying properties. It was very convenient to sit in his new study at Killerton, dealing with Mr. Battishill's almost daily letters, or to invite him to luncheon for a thorough discussion. It was almost as pleasant to receive Mr. Stevens, who—unlike the agent—came in by the 'steward's entrance'. Charlie liked nothing better than to go out with him to some part of the estate where the landlord's judgement was required. Thanks to his hard work with the Bath and West Society he was well abreast of all the latest developments in farming and farm buildings, and, even if in the eyes of Mr. Battishill he was inclined to be a little too liberal with offers of help, his advice was always respected.

Holnicote and Winsford were almost as easy to manage as Killerton. As we have seen, Charlie and Gertie had made Holnicote House their home for a number of years, and Mr. Birmingham was a second-generation steward who had grown up with the job and knew every blade of grass on the estate. Furthermore, John Barton's son, John Acland, had come back from New Zealand and was tenant of one of the farms. Going up to Holnicote was a treat and not a duty, and at certain seasons of the year long visits were made, taking servants, clocks, silver and dogs in the shooting-carriage, while Charlie and Gertie followed in the landau. Winsford, near Dulverton, was also interesting on account of the famous herd of pure-bred Exmoor ponies which grazed on the moor and were rounded up annually for branding and sale at Old Ashway farm. In the autumn they trotted down the lanes to Killerton, where they wintered in the park. Charlie took a special pride in his 'Acland Herd', and there was always a pony ready for visiting children to ride.

Management in north Devon and Cornwall was a different matter. The north Devon estates—which took the collective name of High Bray, but also included some of the most ancient Acland properties such as Acland Barton—had always worried Charlie because they were so small and scattered. He had never felt that he knew them propertly, and had long ago told his father that if any land were to be sold he would part most easily with Loxbeare and High Bray. The Cornish estates of Bude and Trerice were even more difficult because of their great distance from Killerton. Indeed, Charlie often went down to Bude, and was generosity itself in lending Efford Cottage to relations, but the estate problems concerned property development rather than agriculture, and he never succeeded in making the place pay. Trerice, with its beautiful and dilapidated Elizabethan manor house, was even further out of reach, and when sales of land became imperative it was the first to go. Charlie could never square it with his conscience to be an absentee landlord. All in all, the revenue from his 31,000 acres of land averaged out at not much more than £1 per acre at a time when good farm land in Devon could fetch two or three times that amount. The rich 'garden farms' of Killerton were outweighed by the great stretches of moorland elsewhere, while of town property—the source of wealth for many other landlords—there was no trace except for little Bude. The wealth of the family depended, as it had always done, on agricultural land alone.

The Edwardians

On midsummer's day 1905 Charlie and Gertie gave a garden party at Killerton to celebrate their silver wedding. It was a day to remember. The sun shone, carriages poured up the drive, the tenantry sat down to luncheon and tea in huge marquees, and the Yeomanry band played 'selections'. More than eight hundred people walked in the garden and admired the changes which Gertie had brought about. She was a gardening enthusiast in the informal style of William Robinson and Gertrude Jekyll, and she had already made an enchanting garden at Holnicote. As one of the gardeners put it, 'she would sit out there and think for a long time before she decided to do anything or not do anything. *She could see it as it would be afterwards.*'

She must have been longing to get her hands on Killerton, for the late Sir Thomas—regarding 'Garden' as one of the three great 'Gs' of extravagance—had done as little as possible for 25 years, with the result that it was now choked with undergrowth: 'all the ground above the beech-walk was a thicket of laurels 40 and 50 feet high', according to Mr. Coutts, who came as head gardener in 1900. Gertie called in William Robinson himself as a consultant. He could hardly help recommending the wide herbaceous border which was his special trademark, but he also advised a drastic clearance of all the common rubbish to make room for new trees and shrubs and to expose the beauty of the hill. Though his design for a terrace wall to divide the park from the garden was less happy, most of the advice he gave was excellent, and no time was lost in carrying it out. By 1905 the terrace had been finished, the new herbaceous border was stocked with plants, and 'Lady Gertrude's' own glade of early rhododendrons was planted at the top of the garden, to enhance the splendid redwood trees. Many of the large magnolias and azaleas at Killerton date from this period, as do the drifts of cyclamen and daffodils in the grass which give the place its special character. The elaborate rock-garden, made out of the quarry behind the Bear's House, came a little later, when Mr. Coutts had left Killerton for Kew—where he eventually became curator—and handed over his duties to Mr. Wilson, a fellow-Scot. Not all the innovations were a complete success: friends chaffed the Aclands about 'that terrible terrace wall', as Coutts called it, which seemed to begin and end nowhere in particular, and there were complaints about a new thyme-walk where the bees were apt to get up inside the ladies' sweeping skirts. But the silver-wedding-day was a time for congratulations rather than chaff, and Charlie and Gertie must have felt great pride in their new Killerton. It was tragic for them that they had no son to welcome the tenants and join in the jollifications.

For Arthur it was awkward to be a guest at his brother's jubilee, despising it all and yet half envious, with a feeling that the money which had gone out on expensive improvements might have been much better spent on helping poorer relations. Francis, who was now 31, had been adopted as prospective Liberal candidate for Richmond in Yorkshire. This meant giving up a salaried job as assistant director of education for the West Riding ('£200 out of my pocket!' commented his father), and he would shortly face an election which was bound to cost more than £1,000. Charlie, when appealed to, pleaded shortage of cash on account of estate expenses and his social obligations as high sheriff. Furthermore, Francis was to be married in August, and Arthur felt that his brother had been less than generous in the matter of a marriage settlement. Apart from money, there was the question of taste. Elsie, like Gertie, had become a great gardener and had her own herbaceous border at Scarborough, which she herself looked after, dressed like Miss Jekyll in boots, an old serge skirt, and a large apron, complete with bass and scissors; she considered that all her sister-in-law's arrangements were much too elaborate, and told her outright that the rose beds on the new terrace would never do. The ladies were also at odds over the question of women's suffrage. No wonder, then, that all 15-year-old Maimie could remember about the silver-wedding party at Killerton was the prickly feeling of tension between the grown-ups.

Liberal Landslide

In August 1905 Francis married Eleanor Cropper, the brilliant and handsome eldest daughter of an influential Westmorland family of paper makers with Liberal traditions. She was just as keen a politician as he was, and they were an excellent match. Everybody knew that an election was not far off, for the Conservative government was so split over the question of import duties that it was obviously impossible for Arthur Balfour, the prime minister, to hold it together for much longer. Finally he resigned in November, but, instead of dissolving parliament in the usual way, he advised Edward VII to send for the Liberal leader, Sir Henry Campbell-Bannerman, in the hope that 'C.-B.' would be unable to form a Cabinet and that the Liberals would show themselves up as a disunited rabble when the general election inevitably followed. That this did not happen was due to Arthur Acland. He had quite recovered his tone, and was very busy, both in Yorkshire, where he was the chairman of the County Council's Education Committee, and in London, where he was chairman of Bedford College Governors, a member of the Consultative Committee on Education, and chairman of the National Liberal Federation. He had a bachelor flat in St. James's Court, and enjoyed keeping in touch with his old political friends. After Balfour's resignation he was much disturbed when Asquith, Grey and Haldane—the essential trio for the effective Cabinet—declared their joint refusal to serve under C.-B. unless he led the party from the Lords, and left leadership in the Commons to Asquith. C.-B. would not agree to this, and there was deadlock until the event which Arthur recorded in his private journal:

> 1906. On the afternoon of Dec 6 Grey wrote finally to Campbell-Bannerman refusing office—Haldane was acting with him. He (and Haldane) came to my flat and told me so. In 2 long talks that night I urged him to change his mind. At first he quite declined. Ultimately I succeeded. He agreed to go to C.-B. next morning & he then accepted office. G. to F.O. [Foreign Office] Haldane to W.O. [War Office]. A leading article in the *Times* of Dec 7 or 8 had got the facts about Grey right up to the time when he came to my flat the day before—but what happened there when he changed his mind they did not know.

Arthur kept it a close secret and was never rewarded (a tentative offer of Cabinet Office for Education in the Lords was not confirmed), but he had been successful. Campbell-Bannerman formed a strong Cabinet, with Asquith as the Chancellor of the Exchequer and Deputy Leader, and in January 1906 he called a general election which resulted in the famous 'Liberal Landslide', and put the party into power for 10 years. Furthermore, 50 Labour members were returned. There had been nothing like it since Gladstone's great reforming ministry of 1868.

'I am rather proud of my father,' wrote Francis to Eleanor; 'Grey and Haldane are two of the stubbornest men going. I think the Liberals would not have won if they had stayed out.'

Francis himself had a desperate struggle to win the tradition-ally Conservative seat of Richmond with just over 100 votes. He had all his father's intense political commitment and power of oratory, as well as far more physical energy: it was typical of him and Eleanor that they covered the whole of that rough Yorkshire dale constituency on bicycles, and only hired a car on polling-day. 'Where his bicycle won't carry him, he carries his bicycle!' was a saying among the voters, and when E. M. Forster came to speak, and proved to be a non-cyclist, it was a great nuisance that other arrangements had to be made. The declaration of poll was a triumph, and Francis and Eleanor set out on their married life with a splendid optimism which matched the mood of the new government. Liberals everywhere felt as if they were at the start of a new golden age of democracy.

Transformation

It says a great deal for Charlie's integrity that he remained a steadfast Liberal throughout the years of change which followed. By the time he died in 1919 he had seen his Edwardian world transformed out of all recognition, yet, in spite of his great reverence for the past, his loyalty did not falter, and at the very end of his life he showed himself to be not merely a man of strong principles but an actual pioneer in the matter of land management.

The 'unobtrusive diligence and good sense' of which his father had once spoken to Gladstone served him well in his public work for the county. He could be relied on to speak at any important meeting to do with education or agriculture, he was the first chairman of Devon County Council's Education Committee set up under the Balfour Act of 1902 to organise a system of county secondary education, and he had been a leading spirit of the Bath and West Society since 1873. Truly, 'devotion to duty' was no empty phrase in his obituary notices. At home he was 'very much the Squire' according to a farmer who remembered with approval: 'It was—Squire—Vicar—Doctor

—in that order.' He knew his place and expected other people to know theirs. Farm tenants were supposed to come to Killerton chapel every Sunday to hear their landlord read the lesson and to shake hands with him after the service. If they failed to do so, a Killerton groom would appear next morning with a summons to go up to the house and render an account. A stern interview then followed in the study; but 'it all ended with a glass of whiskey!'—to the great satisfaction of the tenant who told this story. Church and estate were one in Charlie's eyes, as they had been for his father and grandfather. The chapel bell still rang to call the men to work each morning, and their children were taught in Sunday School by Miss Stevens, the steward's daughter. The communion plate lived in the butler's pantry at Killerton, and once a month was carried along the chapel path in a baize-lined basket by Mr. Symes, the verger, who was also an estate carpenter. Enormous differentials in the standard of living were taken for granted by everybody. Charlie expected a gamekeeper to come up to the house every morning expressly to brush the dog, yet next to the keeper's cottage in the forest, where the pheasants were reared for shooting-parties, lived a family of children who were so hungry that they came out early to eat the boiled rice and chopped hard-boiled egg put out on the ground for the birds. 'Poor but happy' is a phrase often used by the survivors from those days. Whether or not it was true at the time, Charlie must have believed it.

Until the war came, there was very little outward change at Killerton or Holnicote. Young visitors could still feel that staying with Uncle Charlie and Aunt Gertie was almost like staying with royalty: as one great-niece told the writer,

> I remember the excitement of arriving by train at Exeter, where a footman would be waiting for us on the platform looking very smart with a cockade at the side of his top-hat. There was a carriage and pair outside and we were driven out to Killerton with two large Dalmatians running behind the carriage. As we got near Killerton everyone recognised the carriage and the village men and boys all touched their hats, while the women and girls made little curtsies.

The footman would then blow a whistle as the carriage approached the lodge at the bottom of the drive, so that Granny Baker, who lived there rent-free for this purpose, could come out and open the gate, and the butler would be waiting at the front door without any need to ring a bell. Gertie had a secretary-housekeeper to help her in managing the large domestic staff; Charlie's niece, Cherry Hart-Davis, lived permanently at Killerton and made a charming 'daughter of the house', who could arrange the flowers, feed Aunt Gertie's prize-winning goats, and play the organ for family prayers, as well as help to entertain the constant stream of visitors. Gertie's family—which included a sister married to Lord Clinton and a brother who was Conservative member for Tiverton—thoroughly approved of it all; but 'it was very unlike the Aclands!' said one of Charlie's relations. Not all of them would have agreed. Francis's sister Maimie, who loved horses, never forgot her aunt's kindly interest in her riding-clothes, and another cousin, at the end of a long life, remembered Killerton 'full of lovely things and smelling of beeswax, woodsmoke and freesias'. It was Francis himself who found the atmosphere so stifling, with its huge meals (macaroni cheese, venison pie and apple tart with Devonshire cream for luncheon), and soporific talks with his uncle over the billiard-room fire. He knew that he would have to look after the estate one day, but at the time he had no taste for it. His interest was all in politics.

He had plenty to do at Westminster. When Campbell-Bannerman died in 1908, Asquith became prime minster, with Lloyd George as his chancellor of the exchequer. Francis was made financial secretary to the War Office under Haldane. Arthur was offered a peerage but, following the example of his father and grandfather, he refused, preferring to remain in the background of Liberal politics, where he continued to exert considerable influence. The government pursued its aim of creating a welfare state by direct taxation of the well-to-do, and, after the Parliament Act of 1910 had finally curbed the power of the House of Lords, the pace of reform increased. Lloyd George's budget of that year raised death duties to 10 per cent., introduced a new graduated income-tax and super-tax aimed at the very rich. It also proposed a land tax. All these things threatened landowners, like Charlie, whose wealth lay entirely in agricultural land. In future it would be impossible without making sales to keep estates like his in good order, let alone to hand them down intact to future generations of the family. He had found it difficult to meet the comparatively low death duty when his father died, and for his successor to find 10 per cent. of the value of 31,000 acres would mean parting with a substantial slice of land. The process of erosion was bound to continue until there was nothing left. Charlie did not grudge his estate workers their national insurance stamps or their old age pensions, for he knew that, even under his benevolent rule, their standard of living was very poor, but he always looked on his land as a sacred inheritance to be held in trust, rather than as a mere source of income, and he could not reconcile himself to selling it as if it had been so many stocks and shares.

Paradoxically, the government which had dealt such a heavy blow to large landowners now began to borrow some of their ideas and to take the view that agriculture was in a class apart from other industry. Asquith and Lloyd George decided that it was essential in the national interest to have a coherent land policy, and in July 1912 they invited a small committee of Liberals to 'obtain an accurate and impartial account of social and economic conditions' throughout the country. Arthur Acland was chosen as chairman. It was typical of this singular man that although he continually complained that he was on the verge of collapse ('a great deal of underlying nerve break'), he organised his committee of half-a-dozen men and 70 local investigators to such excellent effect that by October 1913 a report was published which influenced successive governments for years to come. His own introduction was a model of clear thinking and foresight. *The Times* praised its 'fair and reasonable spirit', and 80,000 copies of the five-shilling book were sold before Christmas. Arthur had never expected such a good reception for, as he said, 'it was full of drastic matter and drastic proposals', which included a Ministry of Land, a legal minimum wage for farm workers, state-aided council housing, and compulsory powers to acquire land for allotments. On the basis of this Land Inquiry Committee Report, Lloyd George launched a boisterous land campaign which was designed to form a main plank of the Liberal platform during the coming parliamentary session. Events, however, decided otherwise.

Since 1911, Francis had been under-secretary at the Foreign Office under Grey, whose whole concern during that time had been to preserve peace in Europe in face of the growing threat of war from Germany. Tension increased with every month, and during the spring and early summer of 1914 it mounted with alarming speed; yet not even Francis, with all his inside knowledge, expected war to break out during August Bank Holiday weekend. On Friday, 31 July, Eleanor took her four children away, with their buckets and spades, to spend a month with the Acland grandparents, who had moved down from Scarborough and built themselves a house on the edge of the cliffs at Felixstowe. Francis joined them on Saturday, full of apprehension about war, but never dreaming that it would come so soon, or touch them so nearly. The family went down to the shore and bathed and played games of smugglers on the sunny cliffs. That evening the parlourmaid announced an officer from a nearby military camp who had come to tell them that, in the event of war, the Aclands' house would be commandeered and used as a fort. 'I don't think we quite believed it,' wrote Eleanor. 'We still felt something would prevent our having to mobilise land-forces or even that the country might not go to war.' Next day Francis was called back to the Foreign Office by the news of Germany's imminent invasion of Belgium, and on Monday, 3 August he sat on the front bench listening to Grey's famous speech of ultimatum. By midnight England was at war with Germany. The Acland children were sent up to their Cropper relations in Westmorland, and Arthur and Elsie packed up their possessions and came to London; in Felixstowe the soldiers moved into their house and began to dig trenches in the cliffs where, three days before, Francis and Eleanor had been planning a smuggling-place for the boys among the bushes.

The Pioneer

The 1914–1918 war brought about so much change that it is easy to see Charlie's death in 1919 as the end of an era, and himself as the last patriarchal figure in the story of the Aclands. The reality is not so clear-cut. He certainly typified much that had disappeared for ever, but it would be an exaggeration to say—in the words of the farmer who described compulsory church-going—that 'the war put paid to all of that'. A good deal that was patriarchal survived into Francis's day, democratic Liberal though he was. It took a second world war to make much difference to wages. In 1939, for example, there were still eight indoor servants at Killerton, while table-napkins were bought by the six dozen and washed clean for every meal in the laundry at the back of the house. Conversely, Charlie, whom nobody had ever thought of as a pioneer, took a bold initiative (at least a generation ahead of his time) at the very end of his life.

In *The Times* of 22 February 1917—an issue which carried news of 'The Great Raid at Ypres' and 'The War on the Submarine' as well as a War Office list of 1,620 killed, wounded and taken prisoner—there appeared a letter from the Earl of Plymouth, Chairman of the Executive Committee of the National Trust:

> *The National Trust and Exmoor.*
> *A gift to the nation.*
>
> To the Editor of *The Times*:
> Sir,
>
> We hope you will allow us to announce through your column a very interesting and important gift which has just been made to The National Trust. Most of your readers know that Exmoor is one of the most beautiful of the too few wild places in England which circumstances have allowed to remain almost in their original state. Many will know that a part of this district has long been the property of the Acland family. The present owner Sir C. Thomas Dyke Acland Bart. has for some time been anxious to safeguard this beautiful country, so far as it is his property, from such dangers as might possibly arise in future from disfigurement or injury through building development or otherwise. With this object he approached the Trust with a view to seeing whether the Trust could co-operate with him in a scheme which, without depriving his successors of the enjoyment of the property, would ensure the preservation of its natural features in the way he desires.
>
> We are now glad to be able to announce that the negotiations have been successful and that, unless legal difficulties should arise, some seven or eight thousand acres of very beautiful country will be permanently preserved in their natural condition under the guardianship of The National Trust.

Those acquainted with the district will be interested to know that the larger portion of the lands which come under the new arrangement includes a great part of the valleys of Horner and Sweetworthy, which lie under Dunkery Beacon, the highest point of Exmoor, as well as the farm of Cloutsham, the well-known meet of the Devon and Somerset staghounds. The two smaller portions comprise the wilder parts of North Hill, which runs down to Hurtstone [*sic*] Point, in the Bristol Channel, and a stretch of wild moorland on Winsford Hill, north-west of Dulverton between the rivers Exe and Barle, including the very ancient causeway over the Barle known as Tarr Steps. The whole property is one of very varied beauty—hill and valley, woodland and bare moor—and will be far the the largest, as well as one of the most interesting, and, in the truest sense, most valuable possessions of the Trust. But it will not be a possession in the ordinary sense of the word. The plan adopted for securing the guardianship of the Trust is a new one in its history; one which we believe has great future possibilities for the preservation both of buildings of 'historic interest' and, as in this case, of lands of 'natural beauty', the two defined objects of the Trust. The Trust will not become the owner of the lands. Sir Thomas will grant to it a lease of them for 500 years. With the details of the arrangements we need not trouble your readers. The substance of it is that Sir Thomas and his successors will continue to enjoy the rents and profits and all the ordinary rights and powers of an owner except that the owner will have no power to develop the estate as a building estate and that the Trust obtains such control over the exercise of his other powers as may be necessary to preserve the property, so far as possible, in its present beauty and natural condition.

We desire to express, on behalf of the Trust and the nation, our most cordial gratitude to Sir Thomas Acland for the generous and far-seeing public spirit which he has shown in making this arrangement and for the incentive his example will probably give to owners anxious to safeguard the beauty of places they have known and loved. We have also to express an almost equal gratitude to Sir Thomas' brother, the Right Hon. Arthur Acland, and his nephew, the Right Hon. Francis Acland M.P., who have cordially co-operated with him throughout the negotiations.

The new property will not be a source of income to the Trust. But it will, we hope and believe, be something better than that. We believe that in agreeing to take this new departure, and, for the first time, accept something less than ownership, the Trust is finding a new and useful means of discharging its duty to the nation: and that many generations of Englishmen who will visit Exmoor in the future will gratefully remember the name of Sir Thomas Acland, whose forethought and generosity preserved for them one of the most beautiful pieces of wild country to be found in England.

Perhaps Charlie's imaginative act was prompted by his assistance to Arthur over the Land Report and helped by Arthur's own romantic love of Exmoor, now immensely heightened by war-time summers at Holnicote, but it certainly showed that the 'last patriarch' had a share of the family's progressive tradition. The National Trust, which today is the third largest landowner in the United Kingdom, after the State and the Crown, was then almost in its infancy. Charlie's offer more than doubled the extent of the land under its control and anticipated by over 20 years the 'covenanting' scheme which still remains one of the Trust's most popular arrangements. Strangely enough, it also foreshadowed his great-nephew Richard's decision to give Killerton and Holnicote estates to The National Trust 35 years later. Francis's words were prophetic when he wrote to Eleanor on the day the announcement appeared in *The Times,* after a glorious ride through the August heather below Dunkery Beacon: 'It's really a magnificent stretch of country. Jolly to think it'll all be national!'

POSTSCRIPT

Some day a sequel to this story of a Devon family will have to be written. In the meantime a brief postscript must suffice to show that the Aclands are still as active as ever.

Charlie died on 18 February 1919, three months after the end of war.

Arthur took the title but chose to live in London and to concern himself with his old interests. Until his 75th birthday he was chairman of the Executive Committee of the Imperial College of Science at South Kensington, for which he worked hard to gain university status. He became more and more sympathetic to the Labour party, helping to finance Hugh Dalton and other young candidates in the general election of 1922, and leaving £10,000 in his will for Labour and Co-operative scholarships. He died in 1926 and was survived by Elsie, who lived an invalid life for another seven years, occupying herself with skilful flower painting. Maimie had become a professional artist and was married to Frederick (later Sir Frederick) Bovenschen. They had one daughter.

Francis had settled in Devon before Charlie's death, in order to familiarise himself with the estates, though he did not inherit the title till Arthur died. Unlike his father, he was always a Liberal. In 1915 he had been promoted from the Foreign Office to the Treasury, as Financial Secretary—a traditional stepping-stone to Cabinet rank—and was made a Privy Councillor. However, when Asquith formed his coalition government in the following year, he stood down to make room for the Conservatives in the crowded new ministry, and took the more junior post of Secretary to the Board of Agriculture. Later, when Lloyd George became prime minister, he followed Asquith on to the opposition benches. He remained the member for Camborne until 1922, when he decided to move to his home constituency of Tiverton. Here he maintained a precarious hold until 1924. In 1930 he won North Cornwall, a seat he held until his death. He was acknowledged elder statesman of the tiny handful of Liberals who formed the parliamentary party in the 1930s.

Francis soon became very much attached to Killerton, with a special affection for the forest and garden. He economised so as to subscribe handsomely to Kingdon Ward's plant-hunting expeditions to the Himalayas, and in consequence many new species of rhododendrons made their appearance. He liked nothing better than to take flowers to his friends at Westminster, on whichever side of the House they sat. Eleanor shared all her husband's interests, and was his best possible support in every way. She was an excellent speaker, President of the Women's Liberal Federation for a number of years, and once put up a good fight as Liberal candidate for Exeter. Killerton became something of a Liberal centre, and in 1926 Lloyd George launched his new Land Campaign at a rally of 19,000 people in the park (Plate XVI). Eleanor died unexpectedly in 1933 and in 1937 Francis married Constance Dudley, a family friend of some years' standing. He died in June 1939 and her death followed a year later.

Francis and Eleanor were survived by three sons: Richard, Geoffrey and Cuthbert, a daughter Ellen having been tragically killed in a cycling accident at the age of ten. Geoffrey became a director of the Cropper family paper mill near Kendal, and stood as Liberal candidate for Westmorland five times. He married Julian Fothergill, and they had five sons and a daughter. He died in 1964 and was survived by Julian and four sons. Cuthbert ('Cubby'), worked for the National Trust as a land agent and was the Trust's agent in the Lake District for 25 years. He died, unmarried, in 1979.

Richard, as the eldest son, became the fifteenth holder of the family title on Francis's death, three months before the outbreak of the Second World War. He had been elected Liberal member for North Devon in 1935, but, having been converted to socialism, he led his own 'Common Wealth' party during the war years, advocating common ownership for moral, and not merely for economic, reasons. Because of the wartime truce between the main parties, Common Wealth was successful in winning several by-elections, but it was swamped by the Labour landslide in 1945. Richard then joined the Labour party and entered parliament as member for Gravesend in 1947, after a brilliantly-fought by-election. He sacrificed his political career in 1955 by resigning from the party and from the House of Commons on the issue of Britain's manufacture of the H-bomb and subsequently failing to regain his seat as an Independent in the general election of the same year. He then became a teacher at Wandsworth Comprehensive School, and later a lecturer at St. Luke's College of Education in Exeter—the establishment which his great-grandfather had helped to found.

In 1944 he gave all the land in his possession on the Killerton and Holnicote estates to The National Trust; partly as a matter of principle, and partly in order to preserve them intact for future generations. He married Anne Alford, an architect and the author of this book. At present they live at Sprydon. They have three active sons: the genetic fortune of the family, which has preserved it for over 800 years, still remains as strong as ever.

FOOTNOTES

Chapter One: Acland Barton (1155–1553)

1. J. E. B. Gover, A. Mawer and F. M. Stenton, eds., *The Place-Names of Devon* (1931), p. 342.

Chapter Two: Columb John and Killerton (1553–1728)

1. The date 1554 which appears on the painting is incorrect; it has probably been added later.
2. Inscription in Pilton church, Barnstaple, quoted in Milles MSS., Bodleian Library.
3. W. G. Hoskins, *Two Thousand Years in Exeter* (1960), p. 70.
4. State Paper Office, Royalist Comp. Papers, Vol. X, quoted in R. Sainthill, *Olla Podrida* (1844).
5. 'Whigs' were Scottish Protestant fanatics, and 'Tories' were Irish Catholic banditti: *see* Cobbett, *Parliamentary History*, Vol. 4 (1800).
6. This chalice has now been presented to Bombay cathedral in memory of the Rt. Rev. Richard Dyke Acland (1881–1954), who was Bishop of Bombay 1929–1947. He was a grandson of the Rev. Leopold Dyke Acland (1819–1899): *see* Chapter Six.

Chapter Three: The Peak of Prosperity and the Sporting Squires (1728–1794)

1. A landscape painting of Holnicote, *c.* 1778, confirms that members of the hunt wore blue at this time.
2. Copy of a letter dated 4 September 1759 in the possession of Mr. Napier Collyns, the great-great-grandson of Dr. Palk Collyns, author of *The Chase of the Wild Red Deer* (1862).

Chapter Four: The American Adventure (1770–1778)

1. A number of romanticised versions of the events in this chapter have appeared in print both in England and the United States. Care has been taken here to include only material which can be verified from family records.

Chapter Six: The Great Sir Thomas (1808–1871)

1. 'An account of the Arrangement, Progress and Practice of the Schools at Broadclist, on the Madras System invented by Dr. Andrew Bell' signed 'I.S.' (the initials of the headmaster, Isaac Salter), formerly kept in the Vestry of Broadclyst church, but now deposited in the Devon Record Office.

2. 'P.G.E.' ed., *Annals of Grillion's Club* (1880).
3. Elsie, wife of Arthur Herbert Dyke Acland, later 13th Baronet.

Chapter Eight: Thomas the Eleventh (1837–1898)

1. The Rev. Edward Berkely Troyte was a grandson of the Rev. Thomas Troyte, who in 1730 had married Cecily Acland, the widow of Sir Hugh Acland, 6th Baronet. She had undoubtedly brought property with her as dowry which Berkely Troyte felt obliged to leave back to the Acland family, but his extravagant sporting tastes had made it a barren legacy. *See The Sporting Magazine*, 1824, pp. 56–57.
2. Friedrich Max Muller (1823–1900), the first Professor of comparative philology at Oxford and an authority on comparative mythology and religion. He was a naturalised Englishman and a friend of Baron Bunsen.
3. John Hullah (1812–1884), a musical composer and teacher who introduced to this country the German tonic sol-fa system of teaching singing. He became the musical inspector for training schools and was an enthusiast for the inclusion of music in the elementary school curriculum.
4. Joseph Arch (1826–1904), a pioneer worker for the betterment of farm workers and the inaugurator of the National Agricultural Labourers' Union.
5. Thomas F. Plowman, 'In memoriam. The Right Hon. Sir Thomas Dyke Acland', *Journal of the Bath and West and Southern Counties Society*, Vol. IX, Fourth Series, 1899.

Chapter Nine: The Rising Generation (1842–1892)

1. Rev. Francis Macaulay Cunningham, grandson of the author of a once celebrated book of sermons, *The Velvet Cushion*.
2. Thomas Hill Green (1836–1882). Mrs. Humphrey Ward used him as a model for 'Mr. Gray' in her novel *Robert Elsmere* (1888). Elsie Acland believed that Elsmere, the principal character in this book, was based on Arthur Acland, and in consequence ended her friendship with Mrs. Ward. In fact, however, the resemblance is not convincing.
3. Sommer, *Haldane of Cloan* (1960), pp. 88–90.

SELECT BIBLIOGRAPHY

Manuscript Sources

The Acland papers, some of which are in the Devon Record Office, provide most of the original material, and none of this is separately referenced in the text. In addition the following sources have been consulted:

Burnet Morris MS. Index to Devon Places and People: West Countries Studies Library, Exeter.

Gates Papers: New York Historical Society, New York.

Gladstone Papers: British Library. Add. MS. 44092.

Harrowby MSS. Sandon Hall.

Ilchester Papers: Dorset Record Office.

Printed Sources

A. H. D. Acland and T. Ellis, *A Manual to the Intermediate Education (Wales) Act, 1889, and the Technical Instruction Act 1889* (1889).

A. H. D. Acland and C. Ransome, *A Handbook of the Political History of England to 1890* (1891).

C. T. D. Acland, *Bickford's System of Irrigation* (1891).

J. E. Acland, *A Layman's Life* (1904) (Arthur Acland Troyte).

Sir Thomas Dyke Acland: Memoir and Letters (privately printed, 1902).

T. D. Acland, *Some Account of the Origins and Objects of the New Oxford Examinations for the year 1858* (1858).

T. D. Acland, *An Introduction to the Chemistry of Farming* (1891).

T. D. Acland, *Knowledge, Duty, Faith* (1895).

E. A. Andriette, *Devon and Exeter in the Civil War* (1971).

Annals of Grillion's Club (1880).

J. B. Atlay, *Henry Acland, A Memoir* (1903).

Bath and West of England Society for the encouragement of Agriculture, Arts, Manufactures and Commerce (*Journal*, commencing 1853).

C. W. Boase, *Registrum Collegii Exoniensis* (1894).

J. T. Coleridge, *Some few personal recollections of Sir Thomas Dyke Acland* (1872).

W. P. Courtenay, 'Lady Christian Henrietta Caroline Acland', and 'John Acland', *Dictionary of National Biography* (1885).

A Guide to the Great Exhibition (1851).

F. Hancock, *The Parish of Selworthy* (1897).

A. Harford, ed., *Annals of the Harford Family* (1909).

W. G. Hoskins, *Devon* (1954).

Instructions for Mounted Rifle Volunteers (H.M.S.O., 1860).

J. Morley, *Recollections* (1917).

R. L. Nettleship, *Memoir of T. H. Green* (1891).

Parliamentary Debates (Hansard) (H.M.S.O.).

K. Pearson and P. Connors, eds., *1776: The British Story of the American Revolution* (catalogue of the 1776 Exhibition, 1976).

Return of Owners of Land 1873. Command Paper 1097 (H.M.S.O., 1875).

T. Risdon, *Chorographical Description or Survey of the County of Devon* (1811).

E. C. Sharland, *Ways and Means in a Devonshire Village* (1885).

J. A. Spender and Cyril Asquith, *Life of Herbert Henry Asquith, Lord Oxford and Asquith* (1932).

J. A. Spender, *Life, Journalism and Politics* (1927).

Rev. F. Temple and T. D. Acland, *Report on the results of the West of England Examination* (1857).

G. M. Trevelyan, *Grey of Fallodon* (1937).

J. L. Vivian, *The Visitations of the County of Devon* (1895).

INDEX

For the sake of convenience, many of the entries are grouped in chronological order under the Acland names to which they refer

LIST OF SUBSCRIBERS

Anthony Charles Acland
Colin Dyke Acland
Dr. and Mrs. C. Derek Acland
David Acland
Dorothy Laura Acland MacDonald
E. M. D. Acland
Edward and Janet Acland
Edward Headley Acland
Eric and Lois Acland
Mrs. Geoffrey Acland
Henry Dyke Acland
Hugh John Dyke (Jack) Acland,
    K.B.E., J.P.
James Alison Acland
The Hon. Mrs. John Acland-Hood
John Barton Ormond Acland
John Dyke Acland
John Acland-Troyte, Esq.
Lorna Acland
M. D. Acland
Mark Arundel Acland
Norman E. Acland
Mr. and Mrs. Oliver Acland
Brigadier P. B. E. Acland
Phillipa Mabel Acland
Sir Richard Thomas Dyke Acland
Robert Dyke Acland
Mr. and Mrs. Robin Acland
Sarah Burgoyne Acland
Simon Henry Harper Acland
Mrs. T. W. G. Acland
Valentine Charles Acland
Mrs. Virginia Acland
Sir William Acland Hood
P. M. Adams
Kenneth W. H. Adlam
James Alexander
Pauline G. Alexander

Vincent Alford
B. E. Allen
Marguerite Allen
P. F. and E. W. Allfrey
Viscount Amory
The Rev. J. H. B. Andrews
Mrs. H. G. P. Armitage
Rev. P. F. Atherton
Derek and Nancey Atkinson
Kelly Baggley
Miss C. Jane Baker
Donald R. Barber
D. A. Barry
Mrs. John Bate
Miss C. Hilary Bates
Constance Muriel Bath
Miss Diana Beasley
M. J. Beaver
Phoebe Beer
Gwyneth Margaret Bere
Rennie Bere
Barbara Billows
Miss Marjorie E. Bird
Birmingham Reference Library
A. B. Bolt
John Bosanko
Miss Joyce V. Boundy
The Bowles Family
C. M. Briden
Broadclyst County Primary School
Theo Brown
L. M. Buchanan, Esq.
Bude Junior School
Mrs. Rose Burchett
K. J. Burrow
Professor Gilbert J. Butland
Mrs. R. H. Cameron
Miss Sheila Cameron

Barbara Campton
P. A. Canham
Mr. and Mrs. D. V. Cannon
Marjory Carlile
P. Casley
Geoffrey M. Chapman
Rex Charlesworth, Esq.
Christ Church Library, Oxford
Mrs. J. Clayton Smith
Anna Delicia Coatalen
Ivan Cole
Napier Collyns
Mrs. E. D. Connett
Mrs. Rosemary Cook (*née* Ackland)
Peter Cooper
Carla Cornelius
Peter D. Crabtree
Mrs. Joyce Cronk
Mrs. A. C. Cropper
Mrs. Brenda Cross
Oliver Davies
Mrs. F. Davis
Warren Davis
Mrs. George Dennehy
Mrs. James Dennis (*née* Acland)
Department of Education, University of Cambridge
Mrs. Christopher Deverell
Devon and Exeter Institution
Vivienne Down
J. M. Doyle
D. H. Drake Pointon
Stephen Drodge, M.A.
Major-General and Mrs. Nigel Duncan
Miss R. C. Dunhill
Miss M. E. Dunsford
Mrs. Josephine Edmonds
J. D. G. Edmund
John Edwards Westermill Exeford
H. L. Ellis
B. H. Emdon
J. and K. England
Exeter Rare Books: Exeter
Anne Farewell Jones
Terence P. Farmer
J. R. Farrant
A. D. Fletcher

Professor and Mrs. Charles Fletcher
Stafford Floyer-Acland
Neil Forsyth
Stanley William Frost
Miss J. A. Fulford
Ruth Furze
Lady Gass
Crispin Gill
Mrs. M. M. Gilpin
Dr. Terry Glanvill, T.D., C.St.J.
The Rev. J. W. G. Godeck
Mr. and Mrs. T. R. Goodman
K. V. Goodridge
P. Gould
Comdr. and Mrs. John H. Green
Roy Griffith
Hilda I. Grimmer
G. H. Gush
N. B. Hall
Mr. and Mrs. B. Halliday
Miss Barbara F. Harvey
Miss V. M. Harwood
Laeta Hatch
Margaret Hayne
John M. Hepburn
Colin and Susie Hewitt
Major H. R. Hicks
Jill and Peter Hitchcock
Marjorie B. Hitchcock
E. Hobbis
Dorothy Holman
R. M. Hooper
Miss Rita M. Hore
Mrs. R. Horton
Mrs. Rosemary Hoskins
Professor W. G. Hoskins
D. J. H. Hughes
Joan Huntley-Jones
Ottilie Huxley
Thomas Huxley
Lt.-Col. G. S. Incledon-Webber, T.D., D.L., M.A.
Mr. R. G. Isaac
Mrs. Joyce Jeffrey
Michael G. Jordan
R. H. J. Joy (J.P.)
Mr. and Mrs. D. P. King

Olga Landell-Mills
A. F. Langham
W. F. Laws, M.Litt., F.R.Hist.Soc.
John Lawson
Rosamund and Alex Lee
Peter A. Lee
Mr. P. D. A. Lee
Dorothea G. M. Leitch
Gabrielle Lekas
Miss N. Leverton
William Henry Lewis
Elizabeth Lothian
Rev. A. G. Lough
L. G. Loveys
Audrey Anne McHardy
J. K. La T. Mardon
Mr. and Mrs. Dennis W. Martin
Mrs. Maude-Roxby
Professor W. F. Maunder
Ethel Bremridge Melhuish
J. E. Merricks
Margaret F. Molineux (*née* Ackland)
Rita Molland
N. T. Axe Valley Group
Mrs. A. W. E. Napper
National Portrait Gallery
The National Trust, Cornwall
    Office
Mr. and Mrs. John Neve
Miss Lilian Noble
The North Devon Athenaeum
    Library
M. J. Nott
Mr. and Mrs. John Nunn
Mrs. Winifred Osborne
Mrs. Felicity Owen
Colin Pady
W. G. Parker
R. and M. Parry
Jean Payne
Jeremy Pearson
John H. G. Pell
Nell Penfold
Margaret Pennell
W. J. Perkins
E. F. Peskett
A. J. Phillips

Plymouth Proprietary Library
Phyllis A. Pomeroy
H. W. Portlock, Esq.
D. C. I. Powell
John and Barbara Powell
A. M. Priaulx
R. M. Prideaux
Frances M. Pugh
Gail A. J. Rayment
Mr. and Mrs. C. Reader
John Revill
Jenny and Clifford Ridgeon
Mr. J. K. Ridler, M.B.E.
Anna and Janet Robb
Peter A. Robb
Dr. A. H. T. Robb-Smith
Henry A. Roberson
Rolle College Library, Exmouth
Mrs. J. E. Roseveare
C. V. Rouse, Esq.
Mrs. Marjorie Rowland
Royal Albert Memorial Museum,
    Exeter
Mrs. J. L. Ryan
Mr. and Mrs. B. C. Salter
Elizabeth Salter
Harold B. Salter
Mr. J. Salter, B.A.
William A. Saxton
Dr. and Mrs. D. M. Schlapp
John Anthony Scotland
Frederic B. B. Scott
Mrs. Philip Scott
Mr. and Mrs. A. M. F. Sedgwick
June Severn
Celia M. Seymour
Miss M. J. Shapland
Mrs. Elizabeth Sholl
Simon Sholl, Esq.
A. J. K. and Ll Shubrook
Caroline B. M. Sleigh
J. L. Smeall
W. H. Snowdon
John and Jane Somers Cocks
F. J. Spencer-Brown
Jeffrey Stanyer
Reg. Steele

Eileen Stephenson
Lady Stevens
T. L. Stoate
Catherine Storr
D. I. Stoyle, Esq.
Anthony T. Swain
Mr. and Mrs. D. N. Tait
Margaret S. Tate
R. J. G. Taylor
Miss Eileen Thiel
Dennis and Dorothy Thomas
Patricia Thorman
Jeffery J. Tolman
Sybil Tope
Professor G. E. Trease
J. Tremlett
Mr. Michael Trinick
John Turnbull
Mr. and Mrs. Don. Underwood
J. R. B. Vanstone
H. J. Varcoe
James Lanier (Valletort) Vawter

David G. Venner, B.Sc.
Margaret Wagg
Evelyn Wilder Wallace
D. H. Warren
Anthony Watson
Mr. and Mrs. R. H. Webster
Mr. and Mrs. K. Weedon
Joan Whenday
Miss Whitaker
Mr. and Mrs. H. A. White
S. M. Wide
Charles Wigfull, M.A.
Mrs. Ronald Wild
Dr. Margaret J. Wilkinson
Anne Williams
J. M. Willing
Effie Wilson
B. L. Wood
N. F. Woodhead
Patrick T. M. Woodland
Professor Joyce Youings

HUGH DE ACCALEN, 1155

BALDWIN ECCELIN

BALDWIN ACALEN
of Acalen in Landkey

WILLIAM DE ACALEN = Sara, dau. & h. of
John de la Pile

BALDWIN DE AKELANE, 1321

JOHN AKELANE = Agneta, dau. & co-h. of
of Akelane   Leigh in Loxbeare

JOHN AKELANE = Alicia, dau. & co-h. of
of Akelane   William Hawkridge of
Hawkridge in Chittlehampton

BAWLDWIN AKELANE = Joane, dau. & h. of
of Akelane   William Riverton. Ar.

ROBERT AKELANE = Cicely, dau. & co-h. of
of Akelane   Robert Hawkworthy of Hakwo
(d. 1445)   Tedburn St Mary. Ar.

BALDWIN AKELANE = Joan, dau. & co-h. of
William Prideaux of Adiston

JOHN AKELANE = Elizabeth, dau. & h. of
of Akelane   John Fortescue of Sprideston
(d. 1538)

JOHN AKELANE = Elizabeth, dau. of
(d. 1539)   Thomas Hext of Kingston, Devon. Ar.

Anthony Acland, 2nd son

JOHN = Elizabeth, dau. of
John Cruse of Cruse Morchard

Anthony Acland of   JOHN ACLAND, h. = Margaret, dau. & co-h. of
Chittlehampton,   of Acland   Hugh Radcliff of Stepney
2nd son   (d. 1553)
                           [See Plate I]

Sir John Acland, Kt., 2nd son   HUGH ACLAND, h. = Margaret, dau. of
(ob.s.p. 1620)   (d. 1622)   Thomas Monke of Pother
[See Plate III]

John Acland, 2nd son   Sir ARTHUR ACLAND, Kt. & h. = Elinor, dau. & h. of
(d. 1649)   (d. 1610)   Robert Mallet of Wolleigh;
                                                         remarried Sir Francis
                                                         Vincent, Bt.

Sir JOHN ACLAND, 1st Bt. = Elizabeth, dau. of
(d. 1647)   Sir Francis Vincent, B
                           [See Plate IV]

Sir FRANCIS ACLAND, 2nd Bt., h.
(d. unmarried 1649)

Sir JOHN ACLAND, 2nd son, 3rd Bt. = Margaret, dau. of   Robert Acland, 3rd son   Charles Acland, 5
(d. 1655)   Dennis Rolle   (d. 1655)   (d. 1655)

A   B

Abbreviations

dau. = daughter

h. = heir or heiress

co-h. = co-heiress

Ar. = bearing arms

(ob.s.p.) = died without children

(d.v.p.) = died in the lifetime
of his father

⋀ = branch